ONCE UPON A HOMELAND

LAILA HUNEIDI

DORRANCE
PUBLISHING CO
EST. 1920
PITTSBURGH, PENNSYLVANIA 15238

Dorrance Publishing Co
585 Alpha Drive
Pittsburgh, PA 15238
Visit our website at *www.dorrancebookstore.com*

ISBN: 978-1-6491-3515-5
EISBN: 978-1-6491-3932-0

Every journey is a quest. In 2018, I took a journey back to the occupied Palestinian lands accompanied by my cousins and a friend, who was guided by a personal quest. I returned from my journey with a desire to bear its most abundant fruit in a book, and to devote its analyses to all my readers, whose knowledge about the occupation and ongoing "Nakba," I anticipate, will be expanded upon reading. This book is also dedicated to the Inside-Palestinians—those who have stayed, and live within the original borders of Palestine - who remain adamant, with firm footing, in the struggle against occupation; while maintaining the conviction that every struggle leads to victory

Though our clay is made from our land,
They want us to strand,
They want to destroy our yesterday, and
They still occupy, kill, and bind us today,
They hold us accountable for their melancholy; even worse,
They take revenge by causing us an ongoing catastrophe,
They are changing our demography, our topography...
Yes, they plundered our history, time, and place,
But, we will never surrender our space!

PART ONE

Inception

In the course of the ongoing conflict between two peoples on one land, this book lays bare the abuses of the Occupying Authority and the sufferings of the Inside-Palestinians. Records of such abuses can be found in numerous publications of unbiased historians and politicians, advocating the rights of the Palestinian people as enshrined in *international* law. In discussing the occupation of Palestine and the 1948 Nakba, the initiation of the ongoing catastrophe that forcibly and permanently displaces the Palestinian people, I focused on Yafa. Firstly, because by focusing my case study on one city, I am able to provide an extensive illustration of the prevailing reality as it stands for those living under occupation, a reality that is applicable to other occupied Palestinian cities. Second, to illuminate the past catastrophic incidents of the Nakba and its aftermath, through which all Palestinian people have lost their motherland; resulting in a loss of freedoms and basic human rights. Third, to draw attention to the Inside-Palestinians' inadequate living standards that persist to the present day due to the coercive policies and strategies that are imposed by the Occupying Authority to exacerbate the Palestinians' meager living situations and keep them weakened and distracted. And, finally, to provide my readers with analogous information about the occupation and the status of the Palestinians and their occupied cities, to compare data compiled in this book with previously acquired information from other literature, publications, or media broadcasts.

This journey started across the northern 1948 occupied cities. In terms of their historic significance, those cities possess timeless historical and archaeological value, illustrated in their monuments, shrines, and other ancient ruins. The city of Haifa was our first stop on this journey. Haifa is one of the coastal Palestinian cities that sprang up on the Mediterranean coastline centuries ago. Visiting its sea and wading in its water felt extremely soothing to me, and simply looking into the expanse of blue was a relief. Interacting with Palestinians from Haifa and listening to their challenges informs a substantial part of my research. From them, I learned about the restrictions and obstacles imposed on Palestinian lives and businesses, and the challenges they continue to face on a daily basis while trying to live and work under a discriminative occupation; first as Palestinians, and then as Palestinian professionals and business people.

From Haifa, we drove to Akka, or Acre, another historical coastal city that plays a significant role in both ancient and modern Palestinian history. Napoleon Bonaparte had attempted to penetrate into Palestine through Akka, but his attempt failed; especially after he was defeated by the resistance of the Palestinians and the famous wall which they built to prevent Napoleon from advancing. My visit to Akka was an exciting realization and revision of a historical period that I studied in my early school years. While I was taking pictures of the famous separation Wall that divides the 1948 Occupied Territories from the West Bank, I remembered Napoleon's defeat and the idiom of "Akka's Great Fortifying Wall."

In retrospect, Napoleon's 1799 plan was to defeat the Akkawian Ottomans in Palestine first, and then make his way to Egypt. He hoped that his penetration into Egypt would be smooth and easy after the fall of the weakened, besieged city. However, it was neither smooth nor easy, and Napoleon's loss in this battle that was known as the "Siege of Acre" was tripled. Initially, failing to breach Akka was a downfall for the French military colonial plan and a turning point for French colonialism in the region. By the same token, this setback and the return of the French ships was another French defeat in the "Battle of the Nile," which was planned in Egypt. The French military defeat was followed by a political defeat that overthrew a promise that Napoleon had made to the Jewish immigrants, who at that time were a minority. In exchange for receiving help from the Jewish immigrants to fight the battle of the Siege of Acre, Napoleon had promised to grant the new Jewish immigrants the right to the land of Palestine on which to establish their state. But Akka's fence was a strong bulwark against Napoleon's first attack. The results of this huge defeat resonated loudly in France, postponing French colonial plans in the region for some time, (Encyclopedia Britannica, Siege of Acre)[1].

We made our final northern stop at Ras Al-Naqoura in the Western Galilee. The geological natural reserve of Ras Al-Naqoura has spectacular caves where the sea waves collide with the rocks the most aesthetically pleasing colors and shades one can imagine taking in. Ras Al-Naqoura can be reached by riding the aerial tram over the large Mediterranean rocks. There, we also watched a documentary that authenticated the role that Ras Al-Naqoura played as a gateway, admitting thousands of illegal immigrants into the country.

A few days later we drove south to visit Yafa, Lod, Al-Ramleh, and Jerusalem. In Yafa we met Mr. Abdel Qader satel, a local tour guide, whose parents and family lived through the 1948 war and the Nakba. He was born right after 1967, or the Six Days War, which is known in Arabic as the Naksa. Satel witnessed all the significant past and present incidents that occurred in Yafa, because he was born, grew up, and spent all his life there. While growing up he had advantage of listening and learning all about the Nakba from his parents and grandparents, who witnessed the war in 1948. Hence, Satel is one of the Inside-Palestinians that lived the aftermath of the occupation. His keen observations, knowledge, and life experiences directed him to write and publish a book on the city of Yafa in the Arabic language, titled *Yafa: Fi Thilal Al-Nakba*, which translates to *Yafa: In the Shadow of the Nakba*.[2] which was the first published book on Yafa after 1948. Satel joined us for a sightseeing tour around Yafa's streets and neighborhoods, where he lived and grew up, and came to know all the Yafawian families that are still living there, or those who were living there and got displaced.

Yafa gained much of its character through its location directly on the Mediterranean Sea. Being one of the busiest ports in the country, the port of Yafa was historically one of the most important landmarks for the city of Yafa and for Palestine in general. Prior to the occupation, the city of Yafa witnessed plenty of innovation and advancement of its private and public sector. For instance, its advanced agricultural capabilities ushered in the development of several industries, which accelerated growth in the city. Yafa produced various types of vegetables and fruit, especially citrus fruit. The popularity of its oranges spread through Europe. Yafa's oranges were highly valued, to the extent that the price of a Mercedes car used to be compared to a certain number of boxes of Yafa's oranges. This popularity of Yafa's oranges increased the demand for products from Yafa, stirring plenty of activity in Yafa's port after each harvest season, and increasing Yafa's exports.

Yafa also enjoys abundant water resources, known for its fertile soil, allowing for faster development relative to other Palestinian cities. Its bountiful orchards were not only aesthetically pleasing, but also added an industrial, economic, and social value. Agricultural development yielded industrial and economic developments. At first, factories in Yafa primarily produced agricultural products, but later, they began to manufacture steel. Hence, these factories increased Yafa's productivity, creating jobs and improving the living standards of Yafawians. Because of this, the bustling coastal city became the country's cultural center, attracting intellectuals, writers, and artists from the Arab region.

Jerusalem is another ancient city that dates back to the Canaanite era (7000 BC). That period of thousands of years is depicted in the architecture, sites, memorials, and in the city's diversity, forged by the vast array of its visitors. Without a doubt, the city of Jerusalem is the city of contrasts. It is a center of gravity for people from all over the world, and the focus of attraction for three major religions. Visiting Jerusalem was an unforgettable experience; particularly, watching the people of the three monotheistic religions entering from the same main entrance, and then split, each towards their different zones; a scene that brings peace to mind and heart. It is impossible not to note, however, the strong presence of security guards and heavily armed soldiers all over the Muslim area.

The last segment of this journey was to the West Bank and its three cities; Ramallah, Bethlehem, and Nablus. After the Oslo Accord in 1993, this area became classified as a Palestinian Territory. The West Bank was divided and marshaled by the Occupying Authority into three sections: A, B, and C. Although all these sections fall within the Palestinian Territory, they remained under the Occupying Authority's full military control.

During our visit to three of the West Bank cities, we listened to inhabitants complain about the deteriorating services in their cities. We passed by big demonstrations and heard the demonstrators demanding fair salaries, better retirement plans, and improvements to their health and educational systems. But the Palestinians know that the reason for their low living standards and all their hardships is the occupation; thus, their primary demand is to end the occupation. The West Bank and the Inside-Palestinians are struggling to attain their freedom and their autonomous rule. Although the West Bank is classified, according to the Oslo Accords, as Palestinian territory, the Occupying Authority placed it under its guarded control and has never since lifted any of the restrictions imposed on small businesses, trading activities, banks, and mobility. The Occupying Authority applies various means to uphold a deteriorating situation for Palestinians on social and economic levels, rendering them incapable of attaining true progress, development, or acceptable living standards.

Last but not least, I would like to express my deepest appreciation to all the Inside-Palestinians that I met during this trip, whose articulated testimonies about the Nakba and its aftermath flow from their engraved memories. The Occupying Authority perpetuates the Nakba through its steadfast oppression of the Palestinian people living within the 1948 borders of the occupying state of Israel, as well as in the Palestinian Territories and Gaza. The Inside-Palestinians' testimonies supported the definitions, examples, and evidence offered in this book. The stories that

I was able to collect from real people, and especially those who lived through the Nakba, along with my field observations, have all enriched this work with living sources, which enabled me to conduct an analysis based on well-established ethics and principles of objectivity, autonomy, beneficence, and justice.

In truth, the determination of the Occupying Authority to annihilate Palestinians has in fact been strengthening the resistance, not weakening it. The long occupation years since the war of 1948 have shaped Palestinians' procedural knowledge and perceptions about their future and the future of their children, and affect their awareness and everyday lives. Their emotional and rational connectedness as well as the relationship with their homeland are further confirmed and advanced with each new generation. Moreover, the injustices against them that have been perpetuated for over seven decades of occupation have heightened, and continue to reinforce their relationship with their homeland. This determination is embodied in the new generations' adamance on liberation, and their insistence on their right to return to their original cities, towns, and villages within their homeland.

"Once Upon a Homeland" is a story of a stolen land and its people. It is a story of a land inhabited for centuries by its people, yet gifted to another by a colonial superpower. It's a story about Palestine and how it was disposed and occupied by the Zionist movement to establish a mono-religious ethno-state for Jews. The new occupying power displaced half of the land's native people, and is still occupying the other half and additional areas of their land, as well as gravely oppressing the areas it does not technically control. The Occupying Authority continues its ethnic cleansing against Palestinians, the obliteration of their culture and identity, the authenticity of their land, and commits unremitting violations of their human rights. This occupying entity continues to seize more Palestinian land on a daily basis. However, and albeit the power imbalance, the Palestinians strongly believe that their liberation and return to their homeland is growing more imminent.

"Trust not in your gold and silver, trust not in your high
     fortresses; for, though
The walls were of iron, and the fortresses of adamant, the Most
     High shall put
Terror into your hearts and weakness into your councils..."
                                        —GEORGE ELIOT

The Meaning of Occupation

According to the Merriam Webster's Collegiate Dictionary and Webster's New American Dictionary, the initial definitions of the noun "occupation" and the verb "to occupy" are defined with regards to the workplace, as in a job, place, time, or any space that becomes filled, busy, engaged, or inhabited by someone or something. While in a supplementary interpretation, another association is made to mean "with the possession, use, or settlement of land." The act or process of taking possession of a place, area, or country are synonyms of colonialism, which means "a control by one power over a dependent area or people." While other interpretations for the verb "to colonize" focus on several positive synonyms such as establish, reconstruct, or build a colony. Similarly, the colony in most dictionaries is interpreted as "a body of people living in a new territory," or "a group of people with common interest situated in close association," which can be interpreted as a positive and peaceful entity.

Western colonialism emerged as a practice of policy among European countries in 1488. In its general meaning, colonialism is the external invasion of weaker nations or smaller states by the Western colonial states of greater powers and stronger armies in pursuit of economic interests. The rivalry among the colonial powers had increased since WWI, inciting European powers to expand their territory through invasions, in order to increase their political gains. Following WWII, a new world order necessitated a new form of hegemony and power, as the fight to eradicate colonialism pit imperialistic nations against a growing Third World revolutionary front, buttressed by the Soviet Union. With the evolution of the field of international relations helping to reshape public opinion and educate communities on the plight of people living under colonial rule, colonial powers were forced to reconsider their imperialistic objectives and weigh each theater's importance with respect to their overall agenda. The colonial powers fortified their existence by building settlements on colonized lands, terrorizing and assaulting the colonized inhabitants, dividing them by highlighting their disagreements to create rival factions, discriminating amongst populations of the same religions to implant seeds of sectarianism, empowering ignorance and poverty to emphasize retardation and underdevelopment. The list of the oppressive and divisive colonial practices goes on. In order to maintain their rule and ensure its longevity, occupying countries employed excessive military power against the indigenous populations of the colonized states.

The Arab states that were colonized by European countries are still reeling from the aftermath of the colonial era that tore through the fabric of their societies, and weakened their states, governing systems, and institutions, causing the former colonies to suffer for decades after their liberation. For example, the Arab countries of North Africa that had been under French rule struggled to reinstate their Arabic language, which had been overridden by the French language. Efforts to endorse the original language, beliefs, values, and national identity, and put them back into the educational systems and societies in these states are ongoing. Furthermore, the sectarianism implanted and encouraged by colonial powers lead to civil wars within former colonies. Many of these conflicts are ongoing, as the colonial powers did not only embed sectarianism in their constitutions but also continue to feed it from abroad, long after their rule was over. Colonialism is considered a phenomenon of conquest that reached its peak in the eighteenth century, and ended in the twentieth century. Yet, it is clear that the official end of colonial rule did not end its consequences, as the Arab region still suffers deeply in its aftermath.

Occupation can be defined as a military invasion that takes place for achieving particular strategic gains, it usually occurs over a short period of time. Thus, according to common definitions of the term; occupation ends shortly after the conqueror achieves its goal, such as to force the other government to concede or acknowledge a certain treaty. The examples most commonly associated with the term are Germany's occupation of a northern province in France from 1871 to 1873, and France's occupation, after WWI, of the German region of Bochum. In both cases, the occupying power ended its siege after the two players signed concessions between them. Here, colonization does not apply, only a temporary occupation. Not all occupations can be considered as colonial tactics; occupation, however, is a primary tool of colonialism.

Palestine is currently living under a long-term occupation that has continued for more than seventy-three years. This indicates that colonialism and occupation are not phenomena of the past, as often theorized by scholars in an attempt to vindicate the occupying entity in Palestine, though the practices and policies enacted in Palestine are in accordance with the definition of colonialism and with the practices and policies of the previous colonial powers.

The brutality and crimes of the Occupying Authority against civilians of Inside-Palestinians can no longer be accepted. Their narrative can no longer be believed. Because we are living in a time of connectedness and the instant transmission of information, the inhumane practices of this occupying entity are constantly being revealed, and its continued oppression and occupation confirm this entity's violations of the Palestinians' freedoms and human rights; a situation that cannot remain ignored by western theorists, analysts, and politicians.

However, I presume that the situation that took place in Palestine was not classified as a colonial situation due to the incorporation of the global law of human rights by the United Nations in 1945, a law whose effect remained confined in the national policies of the previous colonial countries, but did not affect their foreign policies. This can be seen in their internal responses to the various transformations of that time, such as industrialization, the changing roles of nation-states, the chronological evolution of human rights that focused on liberation from authoritarian and coercive rules, and the corresponding of human rights to their citizens; while their foreign policies, practices, and violations of human rights remained irreconcilable. That being said, the British government and the rest of the new European democracies of that post-war period did not hesitate to execute and empower the Zionist project in Palestine; although their empowerment contradicted the morals of their political and socioeconomic discourse. Accordingly, the occupation was instilled in Palestine, along with the excessive use of power that violates all freedoms and human rights of its people; thus, with great sorrow, the situation and case of Palestine today is undoubtedly a result of the combination of the twentieth century's colonialism and occupation.

The term "occupation" repeated in this body of work goes in accordance with the interpretation of the tenth edition of the Merriam-Webster Dictionary that provides more specific meanings for the word *occupation* as: "the control of any region or country by a foreign military force that subjects the country and its people to its policies through its military power." Likewise, the word's derivatives that are stated in this book, such as occupying and occupative, are in accordance with this meaning. Correspondingly, one of this book's most employed terms, the "Occupying Authority," refers to the occupative Zionist entity that is still occupying Palestine and subjugating its lands and people to the policies of its authoritative state, government, and administration and to the coercive practices of its different forces and officers, who implement its occupative policies against the Inside-Palestinians.

In view of these denotations, the two phenomena of colonialism and occupation share the same meaning, policies, and implications. Also, under colonialism and occupation, there is often a resort to the excessive use of arbitrary power by the occupying power's army, police, or security forces, who treat the colonized populations unjustly, and use repression and coercion to achieve their occupative or colonial goals. The Arab countries that were under French, British, or Italian colonization still suffer from the repercussions of colonialism. Most of these countries carry residual issues that hinder their progress and development.

Considering colonialism continued with the occupation of Palestine, and colonial policies continue to work hard to keep the Inside-Palestinians underdeveloped, it is equally important for the occupation to keep its neighboring countries underdeveloped as well, with high rates of poverty, weakened educational systems, and high rates of unemployment. The sub-par standards of living keep Arab nations distracted with survival, unable to liberalize themselves or dedicate resources to liberating the Palestinian lands.

Notwithstanding, the changes that occurred as a consequence of the declining influence of the British Empire and the rise of American hegemony transferred the sponsorship of the occupying project in Palestine from the British to the Americans, prompting them to adopt the project of occupation from 1945 until the present. After all, the United States, under President Harry S. Truman, was the first country to recognize the newly formed State of Israel, a mere eleven minutes after its formation. Because of this, many American political scholars defend the occupying entity and obfuscate its crimes by blaming Arab culture for the underdevelopment and lagging situations in the Arab countries, rather than looking at the consequences of years of colonial rule and the purposefully divisive and repressive tactics employed.

This claim had several goals at its core, which will be discussed in Part III of this book, but I am now concerned with clarifying the context in which Western writers used the word "colonialism" to reverse its true meaning: by underlining the theme of development and infrastructural progress, claiming that colonial powers brought Arab countries forward through these developments. However, colonialism was in fact an era of deterioration and destruction. On the one hand, establishments and infrastructures were built to suit the colonizers; construction and developments in their favor, establishments, and institutions in their image. The colonial powers invented several ways to install dominance over their colonies. For example, altering demographics through different colonial policies such as immigration, settlements, and gentrification - bringing into the country thousands of immigrants from around the world to settle on inhabited lands. This is the occupiers' method of creating for themselves a population that they lacked.

In the case of Palestine, the development activities by the occupiers have not brought the occupied people progress or raised the standard of living. And since their establishment, the settlements on occupied territories, built on the razed towns, villages, and neighborhoods, have never enhanced development for Palestinians.

There is no doubt that the occupation is a crime against humanity, irrespective of its attempts to market itself as a progressive democracy that respects the rights of all its citizens. The Zionist entity attempts to mislead global public opinion about its reality, hide its practices, and manipulate narratives, words, and meanings to support its claims. But the fact remains that it is an occupation; a settler colony established on the erasure of other people (UN: The Question of Palestine, Part I).

From a linguistic perspective, by analyzing the Arabic verbs and nouns that define 'occupation,' 'colonization' and their derivatives, the claims of the occupying entity can be undermined. For instance, the addition of the prefix "Esta," or "E-ta" to some Arabic verbs, and "Esti" to some Arabic nouns adds a movement of imposition to their meanings, as in the following examples: "أخرج" "Akhraja," means 'to remove' or to 'go out.' But, by adding the Arabic prefix "Esta" to the verb, it becomes "إستخرج" "Estakhraja" which means to pull out or get out by digging or mining, pulling, or removed by force, effort, or coercion. Similarly, the verb "مال", "Mala," means inclined; slanted; skewed; tilted; or leaned toward; however, adding the Arabic "Esta" prefix to the verb it became "إستمال" "Estamala," which means *was made* skewed or slanted by something or someone's effort or temptation to force it to lean. The verb "أحل", "Ah-llah" in Arabic means imposed upon, enjoined on, but after adding the prefix "E-ta" to this verb it becomes "إحتل" "Eh-tallah," which changes the meaning of the verb to have been taken over, possessed, or occupied one's place, area, or country.

Likewise, by adding the same prefix to the noun of "إعمار" "E-hmar," which means construction, building, or development, the word becomes

"إستعمار" "Esti-hmar," which changes the word's meaning into colonialism, or imperialism, where the building or the construction that takes place under colonialism is usually imposed not in favor of the original people of the occupied country, but in favor of the colonial power and its people. It is a type of construction that follows a destruction of original landmarks, in order to replace them. Therefore, it is a colonization. The Arabic word for a settlement, or a colony is "إستعمار" "Mostahmara;" which is a building that is established to replace an original one, such as the settlements that are established increasingly on seized Palestinian lands.

Accordingly, in both languages, to occupy means to take over a country by the use of force, coercion and repression. In Palestine, for instance, the Occupying Authority is the authorized entity that manages the occupation of all the Palestinian people, lands, and other properties by committing all kinds of crimes and violations. This occupying entity has been using its excessive power to maintain its occupation over the rest of the Palestinian lands by applying occupying policies against Palestine and the Palestinians for over seven decades.

Historical Archaeology: The Land of Canaan

Modern-day Palestine was once known as the Land of Canaan. It had been a well-developed area ever since Prophet Ebrahim migrated to it from the Kingdom of Babylon. The British archaeologist Mellaart, confirmed that the Canaanite civilization unfolded on the land of Palestine during the Bronze era, and described the Canaanites as people who were "living in plastered brick houses, some with clay ovens with chimneys, and even sockets for doorposts. They carefully made small clay figurines of the goddess type" (Mellaart, James 1965)[3]. In the Jewish Publication Society of America, the Jewish historian (Graetz. H. 1891) described the civilization of the Canaanites, saying "The Canaanites became the first mercantile nation through their peaceful pursuits of commerce... the Canaanites were brought into contact with remote nations... they became subdivided into the small nationalities of Amorites, Hittites, Hivites, and Perizzites... The Jebusites dwelt on the tract of land, which afterward became the site for the city of Jerusalem.[4]"

Besides other advantages, the significant geographical location of the Land of Canaan rendered it a center of attraction for various invaders that conquered the land. But many of the invaders stayed and never left. With time, and after years of intermarriages, each wave of newcomers was integrated into the country's original inhabitants and became Canaanites. Among these are the Egyptians, Hyksos, Hittites, Philistines, Israelites, Edomites, Assyrians, Babylonians, Persians, Greeks, Armenians, Romans, Moslems, Seljuke Turks, Crusaders, Ottoman Turks, and others. Together, they developed a flourishing civilization that endured until the fourth century AD. These people were the stock of the Canaanites, who with the inhabitants of Syria and Mesopotamia comprised an ethnic group known as the "Western Semites."

(Nakhleh, Issa 1989) argues in *The True History of the Land of Canaan* that the Philistines, who entered the Land of Canaan in 1250 BC, came from the island of Crete. They settled along the coastal area and established five kingdoms: Gaza, Ashkelon, Ashdod, Gath, and Akron. These territories became the confederation of Philistine states. The Philistines could retain their independence and national identity over their states, but with intermarriages between Canaanites and Israelites, as the marriage of Samson and a daughter of a Philistine.[5]

In the thirteenth century BC the descendants of Joseph and his brothers were led by Moses to leave Egypt for the Land of Canaan, where they formed clans composed of Egyptians and other Semitic groups and called themselves the Israelites. Yet, when Moses died before the Israelite tribes reached the Land of Canaan, his successor Joshua led the tribes in their invasion (Exodus, 12: 38). According to Joshua 12:9–24, the Israelite tribes faced a formidable array of thirty-one Canaanite kings, and they waged a barbaric war, where they slaughtered many defenseless people, as well as animals (Joshua, 8:25–29). As explained by the Jewish scholar of the University of London (Jacobson 1982), there was a devotion to destruct the peoples of Canaan men, women, and children were put to the sword. Their religion and women were source of pollution and showing mercy to them was considered a sin and an offence to the God of Israel; to leave them in possession of any part of the country was considered a source for future troubles because they would lure the Israelites away from the worship of the true God.[6]

According to Nakhleh (1989), over a span of centuries, the Israelites were absorbed into the Canaanite society through several intermarriages between them and the Philistines. It was the power of the Philistines that provided the impetus for reuniting the Israelite tribes. Particularly during the Time of Judges; a loose confederation that was formed by tribal leaders during crises to allow the people to lead. These people were referred to as the judges, or the "Shoftim." Thus, when the tribes experienced tribal divisions, territorial discontinuity, clan instability, social and economic transitions, or external pressure, the Philistines worked to unite the tribes. Because of this, the Land of Canaan came to be known as Phalistine. During Roman times, the name Palestine was applied to the land, becoming the country's official name and both the Greeks and the Egyptians designated the territory by the name of Palestine.

Circa 1100 BC, the Israelite tribes entered the Land of Canaan at Jericho, and in 1000 BC they established a kingdom in Judea that was later divided into two kingdoms in 935 BC; the North became the Kingdom of Israel, or Samaria, and the Southern regions became the Kingdom of Judah. They lived side by side with the Canaanite tribes and benefited from their flourishing civilization. The northern kingdom was conquered by the Assyrians in 722 BC, who took many of the Israelites with them to Assyria. Subsequently, in 586 BC, the Babylonians conquered both Samaria and Judah, and transferred many of their populations to Babylonia. Many Israelites intermarried with the Babylonians and settled there; only a small number stayed or were able to return to the Land of Canaan. The kingdom of Samaria had lasted for two hundred years, and the kingdom of Judah for almost three hundred years; thus, the total period of the Israelite rule in the Land of Canaan was less than 500 years. After the collapse of the two kingdoms, the people of the Land of Canaan became a mixture of Canaanites and Israelites.

The Land of Canaan lost its independence for certain periods of time when it was invaded by the Pharaohs, Phoenicians, and the Assyrians. Various conquerors continued invading the land of Canaan until after the BC period. According to *The Encyclopedia of the Palestine Problem I*, the Greeks invaded the country from 330 BC to 70 BC. They worked on changing the language from Aramaic to Greek, and imposed their own culture and religion on the Canaanites. Their era ended with a defeat by the Romans, who remained in the country from 63 BC until 614 A. D, the period in which Jesus Christ was born and the message of Christianity prevailed. Throughout those years, the majority of Jews converted to Christianity and the country's name became Palestine. The spread of Christianity among the Jews was provoking to many throughout the Jewish community. Particularly since some of them were among the Apostles, whose origins were a mixture of Israelite and Canaanite. These Jewish opponents created a conflict with Christians, but the contention ended with the migration of much of the Jewish population to neighboring countries to escape Palestine's increasing Christian majority.

Circa 613 AD, the Persians conquered Palestine and defeated the Romans. Their victory led to the destruction of many of the churches and temples in the City of Jerusalem, including a severe attack on the city of Eliya. In 638 AD, the Muslim army mobilized to Palestine and began a tight siege on Jerusalem in order to prevent conflict escalation in the holy city of Eliya. The siege continued until the Romans delivered the city to Muslims. They asked for the presence of the Caliph Omar Ibn Al-Khattab, who accepted their call and the call of the people and traveled to Jerusalem to receive the keys of the city. There, the Caliph formulated the well-known Omarian Covenant. Its clauses put emphasis on the safety and security of the people of Jerusalem, as well as their churches and properties.

The Omarian Covenant is one of the most important and oldest documents in the history of the city of Jerusalem and the nation of Palestine. It regulates interfaith relations, preserves the relics of civilizations, and respects all nations and religions, especially the followers of the three monotheistic religions. The Arab rule in Palestine lasted from 638 AD to 1517 AD, with the exception of the Crusades, until the beginnings of the Ottoman rule, which remained until 1918. Yet, under more than 400 years of Ottoman rule, very little changed in terms of the population's identity, culture, language, or religion. On the contrary, Jewish and Christian Palestinians enjoyed their freedom of faith and right to worship. They remained protected, and their religions remained respected. Likewise, as Jewish, Muslim, and Christian Arabs, they enjoyed belonging to their culture and Arabic language, as the Arabic language was given supremacy as Palestine's official language. Under Ottoman rule, the Arabic identity of Palestinians, as well as the other Arab nations in the region, remained more or less respected and preserved.

The British archeologist Kathleen Kenyon stated that the Israelites had failed to conquer all of Canaan, and the Canaanites remained a substantial proportion of the inhabitants of the land. The Canaanites were powerful, and able to influence the more primitive Israelite tribesmen. Moreover, there were further penetrations into the land of Canaan by other Semitic tribes, including the Edomites, Moabites, Ammonites, as were there western and northern non-Semitic penetrations from the sea by civilizations such as the Philistines. According to *The Encyclopedia of Jewish History*, the first Israelite kingdom of King Saul, David, and Solomon was described as a multinational and multi religious state. Its nation was an amalgamation of Canaanites, Philistines, and Israelites. Hence, since its ancient history, the Land of Canaan has remained for many centuries a model of cohabitation and coexistence. Its inhabitants, the Canaanites, some of whom were Arab tribes that migrated from the Arabian Peninsula and Mesopotamia to the Land of Canaan circa 7000 BC, and others who had always lived on the Land of Canaan, fought many invaders. But, when those conquerors stayed on their land to live with them in concomitance and simultaneity, they often welcomed them. Therefore, through the years they became a combination of diverse peoples, who, in spite of their various ethnicities and religions, had lived on one land all together in peace and synchronicity.

This historical account, as cited in Jewish, Palestinian, and other encyclopedias and archives, raises legitimate questions against the claims of a right to the land which the Occupying Authority has asserted since its occupation of Palestine until the present day, resorting to religious arguments to justify its violations and transgressions against the Palestinian people. These religious justifications for political infringements have been empowering for the fanatical groups that persisted in their criminal and discriminatory attacks against non-Jewish Palestinians.

Therefore, to avoid falling into such contradictions, many theologists warned of relying on biblical tales that lack historical documentation for political impetus. Information that lacks documentation lacks validity, and thus should not serve as evidence for any argument. In the Mythic Past, the Biblical scholar and theologian (Thompson 1999) insists that there is always a hidden agenda to building political arguments on ancient myths. It is a usage of religion for serving political ends, an attempt to secure legitimacy to illegitimate political pursuits, or to justify authoritarian policies and practices by claiming them divine; despite, in the case of occupying Palestine, the stark contrast in the Occupying Authority's narrative between claiming secularism and democracy, and relying on a religious foundation and justifications. Therefore, many religious scholars and historians demand an end to the unverified use of religious information, and for a renewal of narrative that includes historical documentation to biblical tales in order to put an end to the recruitment of religion for political purposes.

Thompson, in *The Mythic Past,* stated that articulation is needed to rework the biblical stories that were formulated in the past according to the sway of theologists. The myths about the history of Palestine and its ancient inhabitants were subject to politicization to serve certain political interests. It is the holiness of this land that triggered different groups with different orientations, whether religious or political, to benefit from the skewing of historical facts or the perpetuation of myths. Thompson emphasizes the importance of this formulation of biblical tales on a historical foundation to usher a necessary development that will gradually lead the biblical Psalms and teachings to independence and freedom from biased theology.

Likewise, in *The True History of the Land of Canaan*, John Speller writes, "The beauty of many of the psalms and the wisdom of many biblical proverbs have much greater significance in a global context, where they apply to the lives of individuals today than what has been inferred from these psalms and recruited for political purposes." For example, the biblical psalms about the "chosen people" were recruited in recent history for political purposes, to be interpreted as a gift to a selected people by the Divine to legitimize future practices by their political authority. The "chosen people" reckon they were gifted by the Divine on tribal and religious standards. Thus, when they oppress those who are not affiliated with the same standards, they are rewarded by the Divine who chose them to be above other human beings. This belief allows unjust crimes against humanity to pass without any type of punishment. On the contrary, their conservative believers consider these crimes as righteous in the eye of the Divine. And, here lies the essence of the problem. This belief has become the premise for the discrimination of the Occupying Authority and its proponents.

The Occupying Authority established its state on a foundation of racial, ethnic, and religious discrimination. Religious discrimination, as political discrimination, has become embedded in the state's governance system. It is practiced collectively and individually against all Inside-Palestinians. Despite all the disadvantages of political discrimination, the Occupying Authority does not hesitate to embed religious discrimination in its system and all its institutions, which deepens the divide between the Palestinian Arabs and the Jewish people, and emphasizes the government's partiality to the Jewish citizens. The Occupying Authority allows and facilitates hate crimes that are committed against the Palestinian people either by its police and army, or by the settlers or any other proponent of the government and its policies. Furthermore, a majority of such hate crimes are committed under the protection of police and army officers, as well as the courts. Therefore, the state, its institutions, and employees foster discrimination and support the settler's encroachments on Palestinians' territories, rights, and individual liberties. The Occupying Authority has turned discrimination into a tool that has fixed mechanisms and networks that interconnect with its policies at all governmental and social levels, and it is applied to prolong the life of the occupation, and expand its power.

This strategy has also encouraged further violations against the Palestinians by those who strongly believe that their religious supremacy exempts them from punishment for their criminal practices. Moreover, on a state level, this occupying entity succeeded in imposing its supremacy externally on other countries in the world. It enforced a positive stereo-type around its entity by presuming and presenting itself as a progressive and democratic state, rather than an occupation.

The international superpowers' mode of turning a blind eye to the case of occupation in Palestine in international forums, erstwhile ignoring the perpetual violations of Palestinians' human rights for more than seven decades, has greatly and effectively enabled the Occupying Authority, allowing it to continue its illegal infringements on the Palestinian people, their lands, and their properties. Furthermore, this intentional disregard is a warrant for the occupying entity to act with impunity and regard itself as somehow above international law. It also equips, empowers, and authorizes the Occupying Authority with substantial political gains, which allows it to proceed with its occupation and its expansion plans over additional Palestinian lands.

Documenting the history of the land of Canaan and the origins of its people is fundamental for the Bible's spiritual message, says Issa Nakhleh, the author of *The True History of the Land of Canaan*. It provides the theological field with historical documentation that is crucial to correct the effect of myths about the Holy Land, which influenced the beliefs of some people and their way of thinking, away from spirituality. This caused many to drift toward corporeality. Besides, understanding the history of both the Holy Land and its inhabitants remains an ethical mission for today's theologists and archaeologists.

In 1948, the Zionist Jews who established their new state in Palestine and occupied its land are mostly not Semitic, by the original definition of the word. Today's Jews are either Ashkenazi or Sephardi. Many of the Ashkenazi European Jews left their European countries as a consequence of World War II and the Holocaust to join the new influxes of immigrants that entered Palestine. The Ashkenazi are originally from the Khazars. According to the fourth volume of *The Jewish Encyclopedia*; the Khazars are people of Turkish origin, who converted to Judaism in the ninth cen-tury AD[7]. The Jewish population in the domain of the Khazars was very considerable before they were invaded by the Russians. After their invasion, they dispersed throughout Russia, Central, and Eastern Europe, and later throughout Western and Southern Europe. The Khazars have no ethnic or historical connection with Palestine and most of the immigrants who migrated to Palestine between the nineteenth and twentieth centuries are descendants of the Khazars.

According to Nakhleh, the Sephardi Jews who were living in Muslim countries east of Tunisia are in fact Semitic, and had ancient ancestors with a connection to Palestine, while the Jews of Spain were mostly descendants of Berber Jews who migrated to Andalusia during the Arab domination of Spain. The Palestinians of today are the descendants of the Canaanites. The Christians among them are the descendants of the first Christians. The majority of them embraced Christianity from Judaism during the time of Jesus, and then later, the majority of Christians and Jews in the region converted to Islam.

Palestinian history is rife with frequent invasions that struck the land like storms. However, previous invasions did not alter the land's landmarks and topography in order to dominate the indigenous people and their lands. They did attempt to forcibly expel its entire indigenous population. But in the twentieth century, a great force conquered the land of Palestine with colonial and expansion goals to dominate the land and its people, who lived on it for thousands of years. It established itself on their ruins and started the implementation of its ethnic cleansing strategies that aimed at the annihilation of not only the original people and their history of thousands of years, but also of their culture, identities, and language.

Palestine: The Balfour Declaration from Mandate to Occupation

Zionist leaders' zeal to find a national home resumed during the formation of the Zionist movement in the eighteenth century. The movement focused on strengthening its association with the British, the superpower of the time; fishing for support to secure its goal of creating a Jewish nation-state, particularly in Palestine. In 1897, the movement took its first legal step by legalizing the Jewish state through its public law. Later on, Theodor Herzl, the movement's founder, attempted to gain the approval and support of the Ottoman Empire for his project, but the Ottoman government rejected his request and the movement's purpose of establishing a national Jewish state in Palestine. Herzl persisted until he gained the approval of the British government in 1903. At first, Great Britain offered the Zionist movement 6000 square miles of uninhabited lands in Uganda for the establishment of settlements. However, Herzl rejected the Uganda offer and insisted on pursuing his request for establishing settlements on the inhabited Palestinian lands instead.

After the death of Herzl in 1904, propaganda had emerged in Europe through orators, pamphlets, and newspapers that gave an impetus to what was called the "Jewish Renaissance," and a stimulus to develop a Modern Hebrew language. During that time, the movement's leaders started encouraging Jewish immigration to Palestine, which gradually began to increase. In 1914, the number of immigrants reached about 90,000, of whom 13,000 were settlers living in 43 Jewish agricultural settlements. In 1925, the numbers reached 108,000. Then, in 1933, it rose to 238,000. These first settlements were supported by the French-Jewish Philanthropist Baron Edmond de Rothschild, and from that time forward, the Zionist movement continued to reassert itself on Palestinian lands (Encyclopedia Britannica).

Shlaim, Avi (2007, p. 5–8) states that Great Britain became involved in secretive correspondence processes for two contradictory agreements about the Arab region. The first was for the Husain Mac-Mahon agreement that took place in 1853 and continued until 1916. The second correspondence started before the end of the nineteenth century between Chaim Weizmann and Nahum Sokolow of the Zionist movement and consecutive British Prime Ministers, and continued until the end of 1917. Upon the end of WWI and the defeat of the Ottoman Empire, the British Foreign Secretary Arthur J. Balfour wrote a letter to Lord Rothschild, the leader of the British Jewish community, saying:

> *"His Majesty's Government view with favor the establishment in Palestine of a national home for the Jewish people, and will use their best endeavors to facilitate the achievement of this object, it being clearly understood that nothing shall be done which may prejudice the civil and religious rights of existing non-Jewish communities in Palestine, or the rights and political status enjoyed by the Jews in any other country[8]"*

This letter was approved by the British government on November 2nd, 1917, and published in the press as The Balfour Declaration on November 9th, 1917. This declaration was a gift to a people, but a bleeding wound for another. As a result, the Palestinians rioted in Jerusalem in March 1920, which lead to the death of nine Palestinian people. Prior to all these incidents, all Palestinians - Muslims, Christians, and Jews - had been living together in peace. But, in order to pursue their Zionist goal, the occupying forces carried out hostile campaigns against Palestinians and put an end to what they once knew as peaceful coexistence.

The British government signed this declaration a year after the agreement of Sykes-Picot with France, which was revealed and signed in 1916 to divide the Arab countries into two spheres of influence, mainly between the two colonial powers of Britain and France; except for Libya, which was assigned by the great powers to Italy, which colonized it in 1911. In light of this, the invasion of the Arab states began before the end of the eighteenth century by the two colonial powers of Great Britain and France that spread their influence over most of the Middle Eastern region during the nineteenth century. As a result, the situations of the Arab states deteriorated due to the colonial policies of the two countries that persecuted indigenous populations, restricted their freedoms, deprived them of their rights, and created conflict between them.

The British government took advantage of the Arab peoples' eagerness toward obtaining their sovereignty and unity, and promised to help them build liberated and sovereign states. However, Great Britain at that point had already made and acknowledged its contradictory promise that implanted in the midst of these states an occupation that thrives on these states' disunity, weakness, underdeveloped situations, and intruded sovereignties. Since then, the unyielding support and defense of superpowers to this occupation and its illegal practices has remained on track.

After the Arab states were colonized, the colonial powers divided them by setting borders where there had been none, dividing each state from the other, in order to define areas that facilitated their control over the states and exploitation of their resources. In accordance with this purpose, the colonial powers signed the borders' demarcation agreement of Sykes-Picot that imposed borders on the ground between the Arab states for the first time in their history. Instilling borders imparted the states, embedded disunity, and divided the people of the region. Instead of responding to the Arabs' hopes and eagerness for liberalization, sovereignty, and unity, the colonial powers fragmented the Arab states and implemented policies that only served the interest of the colonizers.

On April 25th, 1920, post WWI, the Allied Forces held a conference in San Remo, Italy to pass a resolution that allocated the Ottoman Middle

Eastern territories to the administration of the colonial powers. This conference ensued into a mandate over Palestine by granting the administration of all Palestinian affairs to Great Britain; which, indeed, was just the other face of the same coin of colonialism, but with a different title. Although the San Remo mandate resolution was held in the name of peace, it was only another agreement for exploiting the resources of the Arab states by keeping them under the "administration," or control, of the colonial powers. For instance, the British Mandate over Palestine had put accents on restricting Palestinians' freedom of choice, opinions, and expression. This was executed by using the force of the British army against all Palestinian opposition movements and demonstrations against the British administration's secretive agreements, as well as the Palestinians' objection to its use of force and oppression against them. Britain's mandate in Palestine ended on May 14, 1948, when the Occupying Authority's state was proclaimed after midnight of that same day. The British Mandate period gave rise to the occupation of Palestine, allowed influxes of illegal Jewish immigrants into the country, caused the death of thousands of Palestinians, and ended with the beginning of the catastrophic occupation of Palestine that instigated the disastrous displacement of 750,000 Palestinians.

According to (Bealey, Frank 2000) the mandate is an authoritative command by a superior country over another. The superior country acts as a delegated victorious country to carry out the wishes of some authorized voters from another country to help them implement certain policies. After World War I, the mandate was practiced officially when the League of Nations put the countries of the defeated powers under the guardianship of the former colonial powers by proxy; on the condition of providing the countries of the defeated powers with help by guiding their governments toward self-governance, which cannot be achieved without developed institutions (Bealey, 2000 p. 202)[9].

Politically, to possess a mandate means to have the authorization of some constituents or voters that represent a government, party, or people to carry out certain policies and make important decisions on their behalf. Post-World War I, the League of Nations assumed this role after the San

Remo conference in order to issue official resolutions for assigning mandatory administrations. The League of Nations was entrusted with granting administrative mandates to colonial countries to manage the states that were under the rule of the defeated powers. Palestine, for example, was one of those Arab states which, according to the San Remo conference, were assigned to Great Britain. Later, in 1920, the League of Nations issued an official resolution confirming the British Mandate over Palestine on the condition that Great Britain directs the local administration in Palestine toward progress and self-government, which the Palestinian leaders were eager to achieve. Therefore, the Palestinian leaders had trusted the recommendations of the League of Nations and the British government to decide in their favor. In addition, they developed good relationships with the British administrators and believed in their ability to guide them toward progress and more developed governmental and political situations. Nevertheless, from 1920 to 1948, Palestine was neither guided toward reformations nor self-government.

The British Mandate was a dual mandate on behalf of both the Palestinian people and the international community, while the Balfour Declaration was incorporated in its articles. Yet, this type of dual mandate had propelled the British government to bypass its obligation toward the Palestinian people. Moreover, the British administration had disregarded the requirements and provisions of its mandate toward the Palestinian people by only endorsing the fulfillment of its promise to the Jewish people and facilitating the development of Jewish political and socioeconomic systems in Palestine. The British government's unconditional support to the fulfillment of the Zionist movement's goal was also regarded as a de facto authorization for the crimes committed against the Palestinian people, facilitating the occupation of Palestine.

During the British mandate, Britain deployed one hundred thousand of its soldiers to Palestine to face demilitarized Palestinians for further oppression; whereas its administration admitted thousands of Jewish settlers into the country, permitted them to stay after the expiration of their visas, provided them with all kinds of assistance, protection, military training, and allowed them to use their weapons against any Palestinian. Yet, Palestinians were not allowed to practice self-defense.

Thus, the British Mandate, administration, and policies were no different from colonial rule. The Sykes-Picot agreement and San Remo conference enhanced the European countries' pursuit of colonial interests in the Arab region, and highlighted the policy of "divide and rule" through demarcating borders, implementing discriminative policies, and practicing favoritism. This policy aimed to emphasize differences amongst Arab populations that lead to racial, ideological, and religious disagreements; particularly sectarian differences, which caused the Arab countries crucial problems. The colonial powers implanted the seeds of sectarian strife, and continued watching and irrigating their crop by sponsoring authoritarianism throughout the region. Hereafter, the consequences of this strategy turned into a tool that was adopted and is still employed by the great powers in several Arab countries for the same old purpose.

The colonial powers' discriminative policies and strategies are also used to keep the colonized people separated to weaken their resistance. This policy enabled the colonial powers of the time to prolong the periods of their colonialism and exploitation. In the long run, through the current authoritarian regimes of all the countries in the region, all peoples' attempts, not only to unite but also to implement any reformations to their political and socioeconomic situations, were curtailed. Thus, the great European powers considered the Arab region as different areas with rich, exploitable resources, and a large sphere through which to expand their political and economic influence. The region remains geopolitically valuable to them, regarding its leaders as political pawns and extracting massive pools of resources to suit their global agenda. The most crucial influence of the geographical factor, however, remains in the location of the foreign occupying body that they implanted in the midst of the region. Protecting it and prolonging its existence is critical to their interests. The primary obstacle behind the frustration of efforts in the region to achieve liberalization and reformations is due to colonialism in the past, and occupation and authoritarianism in the present.

The Nakba:
An Ongoing Catastrophe

There is no crime in modern history equivalent to the crime of displacing Palestinians from their homes in 1948 AD by the Zionist Jews. A foreign minority attacked the national majority, expelled it from its homes, and erased its urban traces, with prior planning and political, military, and financial support from the West and global Zionism ... This is the Palestinian catastrophe in 1948.

—PROFESSOR SALMAN ABU SITTA

Nakba is the Arabic word for catastrophe. The term *The Nakba* became synonymous with the plight of the Palestinians, which began in earnest with the onset of mass violence by proponents of the Zionist project in 1948, and continues until today. The Palestinian peoples' Nakba turned the lives of Palestinians upside down, pushed them into an abyss, and caused them grave loss of life, livelihoods, lands, and other properties and resources; it instigated the loss of their homeland. It is the source of the deep sadness and devastation that the majority of Palestinians have been feeling and living, due to their expulsion from their country, loss of freedom, and other physical and psychological losses and deprivations. This status quo, which the world's superpowers have seemingly a vested interest in maintaining, continues to inflict Palestinians; while its consequences have been passed on from one generation of Palestinians to another until today.

The Nakba is not just one historical incident, nor an event that occurred in the past, but an ongoing present. It cannot be reduced to one occurrence in 1948; it is not only one incident of a massacre, siege, or demolition of houses; it is not limited to any of the mentioned sufferings, damages, or distresses; it is not only the imprisonment of Palestinian children, youth, women, or men; and it does not stop at the doors of the weeping mothers or distressed fathers for their sons and daughters who sacrificed their lives for the struggle. Nakba is all of the above. It is an ongoing catastrophe depicted in a complete panoramic picture that reflects what has been happening to Palestine and the Palestinian people since 1947; it is part of their past and it is still heavily reflected in their present.

The Palestinians who lived through the initial incidents of the Nakba and observed what happened before and during the 1948 war have related the details of what they saw and experienced. They describe how thousands of people were forced toward the sea to take boats from Yafa's port and run for their lives.

Eliyahu Sasson was an editor of a Jewish-Arab newspaper during this time. After he became a member of the Jewish delegation to the United Nations between 1947 and 1948, he wrote a letter to King Abdullah describing the catastrophe that took place in Palestine: "Palestinian destiny has become vague; particularly Yafawians. Since the occupation, they have suffered hunger, inflation, unemployment, poverty, and terror, which made them run for their lives from house to house, neighborhood to neighborhood, town to town, and city to city. Suddenly, their country has become another people's country, and they found themselves homeless and far away from their motherland in neighboring countries."

The crimes against the Palestinian people have not come to an end since the Nakba and the occupation of their country. All the crimes, including killings committed by soldiers or armed settlers, were considered unofficial crimes. Two months after Yafa had fallen, the Red Cross discovered a mass grave with a pile of dead bodies. A Red Cross officer met with Yafa's military governor in regard to the mass grave and was told that the dead bodies belonged to Yafawians who were killed by the occupying Jewish forces because they did not follow the 5:00 pm to 6:00 am curfew. The occupation forces not only killed many Palestinians, but also looted all their belongings. All these crimes happened with the military governor's knowledge, who used to report directly to Ben Gurion, the Occupation Authority's first Prime Minister. In one of his reports, the military governor addressed Ben Gurion saying:

> *"Sir, in reference to your request, this is an assurance that all the ordered wares and articles by our army, navy, and air force will swiftly be sent out of Yafa to be delivered to people in charge.' I would like to inform you that starting from May 15, 1948, a daily load of hundreds of trucks come out of Yafa. The port is ready for the operation, all stores are emptied and all wares and articles are gone." (Pappe,2018, 203).*[10]

In his book *The Ethnic Cleansing of Palestine*, Ilan Pappe (2018) writes, "The greater Yafa area included twenty-four villages and seventeen mosques, today one mosque survives, but not one of the villages are left standing" (*Ethnic Cleansing of Palestine, 201*). The policy of ethnic cleansing against the Yafawians began before 1948. According to the pre-Nakba records, the Palestinians remained the majority of Yafa's population throughout many years, when Yafa's population was 76,000. However, after the Nakba and due to the expulsion of many Palestinians, only 4000 of them stayed in Yafa. Today, the population of Yafa is currently about 60,000, the majority of whom are Jews, while the Palestinians constitute a small percentage after the Occupying forces expelled and displaced the majority of them in order to marginalize and eliminate the minority that stayed in the country.

The British, who left their mortars for the Zionist gangs to use for shelling civilian Yafawians in their neighborhood, facilitated the Nakba massacres. The gangs shelled Al-Manshiyeh and forced its inhabitants to leave. Moreover, they kept all the civilians panicked and terrified through arbitrary bombings of the streets and the buildings of Yafa with barrels of explosives. They killed many people by bombing places that used to attract crowds, such as Nozha Street and the Sarai building.

In Yafa alone, the members of the Zionist organizations committed eighteen famous massacres. Many Palestinians died due to shootings, assault, rape, and oppression. For instance, in villages, members of Zionist militias tore through pregnant mothers' wombs to kill the mothers and their babies. These crimes are documented with more information and pictures in *The Encyclopedia of the Palestine Problem, I & II, 1991*. The aim behind these brutal crimes was not only to achieve the expulsion and forced eviction of Palestinians, but also to terrorize the population, prolong their relegation, keep them in exile, and confiscate their properties.[11]

The ongoing catastrophe, or the Nakba, continues to affect the lives of Palestinians, who are still suffering from its repercussions, whether the Inside-Palestinians or the diaspora. And this devastating disaster continues to cause havoc to the future of Palestinian youth, who remain deprived of their homeland and all their rights. However, attempts to deny this crime continue at all levels. On the political level, for example, the positions of powerful countries on the Palestinian issue have not changed. Rather, they oscillate from bad to worse. On the economic level, various financial and economic pressures continue on the Inside-Palestinians to impoverish the rest of them, with the aim of achieving two goals. First, to exhaust them and end their ability to resist the occupation. Second, to force them to leave their cities or villages and emigrate outside their country. In light of the increasing political and economic challenges, social challenges are also increasing. Educational levels, employment opportunities, and access to the most basic elements of a decent life are difficult to come by, in addition to an ongoing struggle to protect the Arab identity and preserve their Palestinian values and culture from the attempts of obliteration by the Occupying Authority.

As for the displaced Palestinians, their suffering is no less than that of those who remain under occupation. Under such circumstances, all Palestinian people are challenged regardless of the peculiarities and conditions of the places they ended up. The common denominator remains the occupation that took over their homeland and left them without one; including the Palestinians, who live in the diaspora under better conditions. The truth of the matter is, all the Palestinian people are collectively suffering, and have been since 1948.

According to Satel's book, during the chaos of the Nakba and on the first day of the 1948 war, there was blood in every corner of Yafa. The Zionist militias were on a mission to raise the level of fear among Palestinian families by creating frightening sounds from various missiles and scattering blood and body parts everywhere to disseminate horrific scenes and the smell of death. They planted explosives to kill more civilians. These scenes were concentrated around the Al-Manshiyeh neighborhood, which was one of Yafa's most populated neighborhoods. Zionist militia members had rigorously focused on killing civilian men to scare their families and encourage them to escape when they saw the dead bodies of their fathers or husbands. Also, these gangs placed concealed snipers over Yafa's tall buildings in attempts to scare more families and force them to run away.

All this occurred with the complete absence of the military leadership of the British Mandate, its police, and its administrators, who withdrew from all centers, police stations, and government buildings to allow this chaos and the occupying entities to have control over the country. According to these testimonies, the withdrawal of the British forces was secretive, abrupt, and complete. For that reason, the British withdrawal from Palestine on May 14th, 1948, was part of the occupation plan. Thus, the British forces had deliberately left hundreds of thousands of unarmed Palestinian civilians without protection or shelter to suffer the tyranny, aggression, and injustice of internal and external fully armed invaders.

In *The Ethnic Cleansing of Palestine*, Pappe described this particular scene, saying the people were literally pushed into the sea when crowds tried to board the small fishing boats to escape gunfire by the Jewish troops to hasten their expulsion. After the fall of Yafa, the occupation of Jewish forces initiated the depopulation of all major Palestinian cities and towns, many of whose inhabitants never saw their homeland again.

The sight of people jostling to board small boats in search of safety for families was described by many through word of mouth, poetry, or depicted in portraits. Satel described this scene by saying, "During the war, Yafa's Port was overcrowded; not with goods, parcels, and orange boxes as it used to be, but with scared people running away from the prevalent atrocities all over Yafa."

There, at the port, families took the small fishing boats without knowing where they would sail, or at which port they would dock. Some boats took people south to Gaza, or further to Egypt, while others sailed north to Lebanon and Syria. It was a dreadful scene, a chaotic stampede with families split apart, children lost, and a terrified population escaping towards an unknown future. They did not realize that the moment they put their feet in the boats, they would never be allowed to return to their homeland. The brutal crimes and atrocities of the Occupying Authorities' occupying forces and its proponents were committed with a dual goal; to annihilate a large number of Palestinians, and to displace even larger numbers of them. The occupying forces disseminated violence in and around numerous cities and villages to expedite the eviction of their inhabitants. The threatening and intimidating situations occurred particularly in the coastal cities that have ports or departure gateways, such as Haifa and Yafa. The chaos that took place in Yafa, for instance, triggered many of its families to seek safety and security elsewhere. Yafa's stampede was depicted by several artists, who drew Yafa's port during the war and how it was huddled with people. These artists used their paintbrushes to depict the impact of the atrocities and bloodshed on the Yafawian families. They drew them running toward the sea with their back to their city, rushing their family members to get away from the bloodshed, and attempting to squeeze themselves in small fishing boats with expressions of fear on their faces.

This scene was transformed by Tamam Al-Akhal, an artist from Yafa, who conveyed an alternative image in one of her paintings. Instead of depicting the reality of people running toward the sea with their backs to Yafa, she painted them with their backs to the sea, moving towards Yafa instead. She wanted her Palestinian subjects to be returning to Yafa, not departing it. She drew secure and confident expressions rather than fearful ones on their faces, as though she is saying "No more fear and no more displacement for Palestinians, because the return is factual and inevitable." In her painting, Tamam Al- Akhal depicted the imagination of so many Palestinians.

During the chaos in Yafa, the Occupying Authority had aimed to open the city of Yafa for thousands of new immigrants to replace its original inhabitants, but several Yafawian families refused to submit to the desires of the occupation and its administration and considered the submission to this policy a betrayal. Principally, any submission or cooperation with the occupiers is still considered as collaboration with the enemy by the majority of Palestinians. However, the brutality of these gangs and militias obligated a group of Yafa's senior chiefs to accept the transformation of Yafa into an open city in exchange, as they demanded, to cease all atrocious crimes against civilians.

All military committees in Palestine were appointed by the British Mandate. Throughout the anarchical situation prior to and during the 1948 war, none of these committees had received directives from the mandated military leadership, but on the contrary, were left without any guidance from the military commandment. The following published letter by Michel Al-Issa, a military commander in Yafa, and Fawzi Al-Qawuqji, a member of the Military Committee, portrays the chaos that was intended and planned by the British Mandate prior to the onset of the 1948 war. According to Satel (2018 p. 200) Al-Issa wrote the following letter to inform the Military Committee about the crimes of the occupying gangs, and to put in plain words the impact of these crimes on Yafa and the lives of Yafawians. The letter describes how the civilians people reacted to these violent situations, which they found themselves facing alone:

> "The whole garrison escaped. A big group of it escaped from
> Ajnadeen leaving Yafa in the hands of occupying armed gangs
> that controlled the road to Yafa, Ramleh, and Jerusalem. These
> gangs are terrifying civilians with killing and bloodshed; creating

disastrous sites around Yafa to horrify people and trigger them to run away, evacuate their homes, close their stores, and leave their city. Everything is shut down, even bakeries. Yafa is left without protection and its houses and shops are getting looted by the gangs. Yafa's hospitals were rendered without doctors; only twenty percent of doctors and staff stayed in one hospital, while all others escaped, leaving their patients unattended. There are piles of dead bodies everywhere and there is no one in the graveyards to bury them. We are living in turmoil! This is an urgent request for immediate assistance; awaiting your prompt reply or further instructions."

The two well-known massacres of Deir Yassin, located west of Jeru-salem, and Kufur Qasem, just outside Yafa, were soon committed, in which the inhabitants of the two towns were collectively slaughtered. Both atrocities were carried out by the same militias and border guards, which later and after the establishment of the new occupying state, were officially adopted into the security apparatus by the Occupying Au-thority's government (Pappe, 2006. P. 232–302).

The Atrocious Offensive Role of Zionist Organizations During the 1948 War

The endeavor of the leaders of the Zionist organization, allegedly to establish a homeland for the Jewish people in Palestine, was a major factor in this war. Yeshayahu Ben Fort, a Knesset member, said "There is no Jewish state without the eviction of Arabs from Palestine, the confiscation of their lands, and fencing them." This became the Occupying Authority's philosophy for constructing settlements on embezzled Palestinian lands, in line with the phrase of "a land without a people for a people without a land" that was associated with the Zionist movement to justify its establishment of a Jewish homeland in Palestine, and which has become a widely cited phrase during the 19th and 20th centuries.

During the British Mandate, the number of Zionist organizations in Palestine rose, the influx of illegal Jewish immigrants increased, and the magnitude of settlement construction multiplied. The Mandate government played a major role in enabling the Jews to control large swaths of Palestinian lands. Thus, the Zionist leaders considered the British Mandate's facilities a great advantage to the fulfillment of their project. Britain remained committed to the Balfour Declaration, and amongst its most important facilities, the British Mandate maintained the construction of settlements under its protection and supervision. For the indigenous population who lived under the mandate, it was quite the reverse. The British army used its power to subjugate them to its policies by force; a position no different than that of indigenous populations in most British colonies. This highlights the fact that the mandate is merely another phase, or version, of colonialism; they are different titles, but virtually the same systems of oppression. Under its mandate, the British forces committed severe violations of the rights of Palestinians, levied serious restrictions on their freedom of expression by suppressing their demands for freedom and self-governance, and diverged entirely from what the mandate had stipulated. Instead of assisting the Palestinians to improve governance and enhance political and economic institutions to achieve autonomy, the British government facilitated and empowered a coercive and expansive occupation on inhabited lands that caused a human catastrophe that is ongoing today. In order for the British government to keep its influence on the whole region during that time and for the future through this occupation, it ignored the existence of the Palestinians, their self-determination, their rights within their own country, and their basic human dignity.

Under the British Mandate, the Palestinians were prevented from defending themselves against attacks by armed settlers. This policy was aimed at rendering the Palestinians vulnerable, ineffective, and defenseless in order to weaken their ability to resist the growing occupation. British officials considered Palestinian self-defense against attacks by armed settlers illegal and imposed a penalty amounting to death for attempting any means of resistance.[12]

The 1948 war broke out between two unequal forces. Especially when the British mandate had surreptitiously allowed the entrance of many fighters from different countries. Both the implanted fighters and the members of Zionist organizations were proficient, trained, and armed with modern weapons. The foreign fighters were made up mostly of individuals who had fought with the British Army during World War II. They were brought in to bolster the Zionist organization's various militias and to exacerbate and diversify the violence perpetrated on the people of the land.

The Palestinian resistance that emerged in response was made up of civilian volunteers who lacked training, information, and weapons. Yet, in spite of the wide gap of power, the Palestinians did not shirk from defending their lands, and have not stopped since, despite the numbers killed and displaced, generation after generation. Since the 1948 war, the number of martyrs among Palestinians continues to rise. The formation of covert Zionist gangs inside Palestine had been in progress since 1909, and increased after the British Mandate undertook the administration of the country. These gangs developed into organizations, essentially militias, and their criminal activities against Palestinians continued, including the recruitment and training of members from the recently arrived settlers. These activities were run behind the fences of the settlements that were established as a residence for thousands of illegal visitors, whose visit visas, offered by the British administration, had long expired. They were, however, allowed to remain in the country and to reside in the settlements that were built to accommodate them.

According to a study by Aljazeera Research Center, "The War of 1948," the first of these gangs, which evolved into an organization, was the Hashomer gang, established in 1909, which later became the secret military organization of the Zionist movement. The Haganah gang was then established in Jerusalem in 1921 with the mission of training and defending new immigrants. Among its tasks was to establish fifty settlements in different areas in Palestine, and to facilitate illegal immigration into the country.

The Ergon was established in 1931 by the Russian Ebrahim Tihomi, whose resentment against Palestinians was expressed in several vicious crimes against them committed by the Ergon members. This organization refused to limit its murderous crimes and committed over sixty military attacks against Palestinians. It also started attacking different British centers. The Ergon was receiving periodic subsidies from the Polish government, which was encouraging Jewish emigration to Palestine from 1936. The Ergon, difficult to control, was classified by the British as a terrorist organization. But in 1943, the Ergon was headed by Menachem

Begin, who, afterward, became the Prime Minister of the Occupying Authority's government. The Ergon, then, was combined with other Zionist military organizations to form the Occupying Authority's so-called Defense Army.

The Shtern organization was founded in 1940 by a Jewish immigrant from Poland by the name of Abraham Shtern, who wanted to work independently outside the scope and directives of the Zionist Organization, the Haganah, and the British Mandate. This organization was focused on ending the British Mandate in Palestine to replace it and announce their occupation of the country. It was one of the most famous and fierce organizations that participated in several massacres, such as the Massacre of Sa`sa, Bilad al-Sheikh, where they blew up many homes in the two villages and killed people. They also lead the massacre of Deir Yassin, west of Jerusalem, in 1948, committed with the goal of ethnically cleansing it of Palestinians, and wiping the village off the map. The Shtern organization was also dissolved into the Occupying Authority's army, and honored by granting some of their members the title and badges of "State Warriors."

Yithak Sadie, a former officer in the Tsarist Russian army, founded the Palmach. Moshe Dayan, who became Minister of Defense, Yitzhak Rabin, who became Prime Minister, Yigal Allon, who became Deputy Prime Minister, and the former President Ezra Weizmann were all also among Palmach's early founders. The Zionist organization began operating on May 19, 1941. It was known by the nickname, "Soldiers of the Storm," and became the striking arm of the Haganah. The Palmach was incorporated into the Occupying Authority's chief military apparatus, by the Occupation's first Prime Minister, Ben Gurion. It committed several crimes, such as the bombing of railway lines, and was known for its sudden raids on different Palestinian villages to spread horror. The Palmach encompassed nine teams, who received arduous training in the acts of blowing up and suddenly attacking peaceful civilians at their homes during night raids. This organization had also attacked the British to accelerate the fulfillment of the Zionist project. The Palmach also ran well-organized intelligence operations that infiltrated German camps for the purposes of espionage and sent members undercover as Arabs to settle in Syria and Lebanon for the same purpose.

After the Palestinians began to revolt in 1936, an uprising which later came to be known as The Great Revolt (al-Thawra al- Kubra) or The Great Palestinian Revolt (Thawrat Filastin al-Kubra), a nationalist uprising by Palestinian Arabs in Mandatory Palestine against the British administration of the Palestine Mandate, demanding Arab independence and the end of the policy of open-ended Jewish immigration and land purchases, the Haganah trained many young extremists in its ranks until they attained 1000 fighters with 4000 well-trained reservists. All the Haganah fighters were employed to suppress the Palestinians who demonstrated a demand for any of their rights or resisted the degrading conditions and standards of living. The cooperation between the British mandate and the Zionist project extended to all levels, until the Zionist organizations decided to accelerate the founding of their illegal state by ending the British Mandate, and initiating their sole occupation over the country.[13]

In light of this situation and the great difference in the balance of power, the Palestinian resistance that emerged was unable to stop the bloodshed, battle with the Zionist organizations, or respond adequately to their intensive and violent attacks. Nor were they able to protect their people from eviction or save their properties from confiscation. Still, the Palestinians were determined to defend their homeland. They had high hopes for receiving support and ending this fierce war in their favor, but the occupation's capabilities remained much bigger than their hopes and aspirations.

PART TWO

PART TWO

Yafa: The Sentimental City of Palestine

In his book on Yafa, rife with longing, Satel writes:

> *"A common symbol associated with the city of Yafa is the orange tree. While citrus trees, in general, are reminiscent of Yafa's character and history, the orange tree holds a special place for Yafawians and those who come into its harbor. Yafa's past is indeed akin to the delicious, tart taste of its citrus fruits. The scent and taste of Yafa's oranges linger at the forefront of Palestinian collective memory. Savoring Yafa's sweet, luscious oranges transports dispersed Palestinians worldwide back to their homeland. The roots of Yafa's citrus trees plunge into the depths of Yafa's ancient history, and the begotten buds on its branches correspond to the blossoming of Yafa's promising new generations. Every orange tree in Yafa bears witness to its history. In the retaining memory of every Yafawian there is a heartbroken aged man beneath Yafa's orange trees, shaking his cane at the audacious aggressors in a futile attempt to stop them from hurting his motherland. Yafa remains the spring of love to all her devoted children. This relationship between Yafawians and their citrus trees is parallel to their relationships with their real mothers. They feel blessed because their motherland loves them all equally, whether they are present or forcefully absent. Accordingly, Yafa's orange trees are the liaison that consolidates*

its people, connects them with others, links them with time, and adheres them to their land. Yafa is the time and the place; Yafa is the homeland." (Satel, 2018, 3)

In the eyes of Yafawians and other Palestinians, the city of Yafa is not like any other city. It is a symbol of pride, dignity, luxurious life, and prosperity of knowledge and sciences. Sadly, after the Nakba, this image was replaced; after the catastrophe, Yafa's story was tainted with sorrow. It came to represent the initiation of the Nakba and the horrors that befell it and its surrounding towns and villages. Handala, a cartoon created by Naji Al Ali from 1975–1987 depicted the complexities of the plight of Palestinian refugees. The barefoot refugee child with his back turned remains a potent symbol of the Palestinian struggle and fight for justice and self-determination.[14]

Before the occupation, Yafa was Palestine's metropolitan city that attracted all other Palestinians to its groves, shores, and its bustling port, which made Yafa an international gateway. Thus, the city boasted cultural centers, theaters, cinemas, and multiple markets. Yafa's beauty was augmented by its coast and its famously fertile lands. It was both a coastal and an agricultural city, full of orchards that spilled into its streets. The Yafawians still remember the famous theaters of the Nabil Cinema and Cinema Rashid that continued to operate for some time until they were confiscated from the Palestinians by the Occupying Authority. Both cinemas were incredibly lively and would screen films from across the region and the world. The Nabil Cinema was made into a commercial theater with a capacity of 1200 seats, and Rashid Cinema was turned into an event venue, but Palestinians are prohibited from entering or renting them.

Palestinians still associate the lands with the names of the Yafawian families who owned those lands. One such example is the current site of Yafa's post office, built on a lot that was owned by the Abu Khadra family, whose members owned various properties around the area of Yafa and Tel Aviv. The post office building is still there, but the land on which it stands was confiscated by the Occupying Authority. Those who were born in Yafa and know its neighborhoods, streets, establishments, and landmarks, are witness to the many alterations and demolitions that have been imposed on its landscape and urban fabric over seventy-two years of occupation. Some places were entirely confiscated and altered, others, such as the famous Sarai building, were destroyed by bombing. Similarly, many private and public properties were completely demolished and replaced; many alterations were established to disconnect certain areas, and connect others.

The Yafawians called their city "The Mermaid of the Sea," "The Welcoming City," or "يافا إم الغريب" meaning "The Mother of the Stranger," amongst many other names. Undoubtedly, Yafa the mermaid of the Mediterranean Sea is the mother of all strangers. Yafa accepted the droves of foreigners that landed on its shores, embraced them, and welcomed them among its people. In his book, Satel shares a story that illustrates the extent to which the Occupying Authority is set on erasing Palestinian memory of their homeland; "After I finished high school, I expressed my passion to Yafa by composing some poetic verses to convey my feelings about my city and country, but my poems prompted the Occupying Authority's Intelligence Service to recall me for investigation." He added that the Occupying Authority's coercive power does all that it takes to put a curb on Palestinians' creativity and halt their growth, and said that "since the Nakba, the Occupying Authority has been nipping the Palestinian buds from growing, hindering their developmental efforts, and thwarting their progress."

Displacement: A Transfer from Security to Insecurity

The displacement of a population requires forced transfer from one place to another without regard to the location, position, or condition the displaced population ends up in. The occupying forces invaded Palestine after conducting a covert illegal immigration strategy by submerging the Palestinians and their land with an implanted population and then alleging the immigrants' historical affiliation with Palestinian land. As mentioned, the occupying forces that planned for the occupation of Palestine for many years ahead implemented its occupation under the auspices and support of colonial powers, thus, the occupying forces were allowed to commit crimes and violations against the disarmed Palestinian civilians and their country. The colonial powers' support for the process allowed the severe displacement of an indigenous population and enabled the formation of an illegal occupation bolstered by a new immigrant population that adopted a religious and political ideology; becoming the core political and social proponents of the Occupying Authority.

Those who have an affiliation with the land of Palestine - Jews, Christians, and Muslims - have always been a part of Palestine's population. They are the indigenous inhabitants of the land and their existence in Palestine dates back thousands of years, through many civilizations and mass religious conversions. By the time the occupation began in earnest, Palestine's indigenous population was comprised of a Muslim majority.

The Zionist project depended on the displacement of large numbers of Palestinians who lived in coastal cities and their surrounding villages, as these locations allowed for an exodus from the sea. The Palestinians residing there would be forced to leave the country entirely, rather than become internally displaced. Having operational ports helped facilitate the implementation of this plan. 96% of Yafa's inhabitants were coerced to leave their homeland by sea to escape violence. The people of Yafa were hopeful that their evacuation would not last aspired to return quickly to their beloved city as they were promised by various Arab leaders of the time, who promised to help the Palestinian people to return to their homeland. The Yafawians considered these promises viable and believed in their eventual return.

Satel described the incidents that preceded the displacement of many Yafawians saying it was "...as if everything was put inside a black box and buried because the Occupying Authority was keen on keeping their vehement crimes and practices unrevealed." Those few who managed to remain in Yafa watched the violent mutation of their city in horror.

The exact number of Palestinians who were killed during the 1948 Nakba remains unknown. Those who were forced into exile through the ports or across the Jordan River number to approximately 700,000 Palestinians. Many perished on their journey to the unknown, drowning in the Mediterranean, dying of thirst in the desert, or crushed by one of the many stampedes that occurred in the chaos. Those who survived were displaced to other Palestinian cities or neighboring countries. Nonetheless, most ended up as refugees, living in refugee camps under horrific conditions.

During the 1948 war, many Yafawians also suffered from the disappearance of their loved ones. Amidst the chaos, violence, and exodus, many families were split and individuals vanished. Their loved ones were left without any information or guidance. Eventually, some families were informed that their missing family member(s) were in prison or pronounced dead. Similarly, hundreds of martyrs were buried in mass graves discovered in 2013 during a dig by, announced by the Al-Aqsa Foundation for Endowment and Heritage.

The Yafawians who stayed in Yafa were displaced in their own city; they were rounded up and forced by the Occupying Authority to live in a specific area reserved for them. These areas resembled the Jewish ghettos of European countries. Thus, this area became known as "The New Ghetto," and was the sole designated area for displaced Yafawians, forced to live under the Occupying Authority's military rule. The ghetto was isolated from the rest of Yafa by a surrounding barbed wire fence. The inhabitants' movement was also limited by restrictions put in place by the New Ghetto's Military Governor, whose permission was needed to permit Yafawians to leave the area.

Many of the displaced Yafawians have continued to suffer greatly. For instance, after the demolition of the entire Al- Manshiyeh neighborhood, its inhabitants sought refuge in the old Ajami neighborhood by staying in its emptied houses. Yet, they were forced again to move out. According to Satel, his family was forced to relocate several times; first they were displaced from Abu-Kabeer to the old Ajami. Once they began to settle, they were moved to the New Ajami, or the New Ghetto, where life was terribly oppressive under the Occupying Authority's rule. Yet they were compelled to tolerate and abide by all restrictions in order to stay in their city.

The Occupying Authority has been known to exert all efforts to expel the remaining Yafawians and force them to leave not only their homes, but also their shops and businesses. Thus, it deploys harassment tactics against Yafawian businesses to pressure them into leaving; but many of these Yafawian owners have been resisting the Occupying Authority's harassments and tolerating the unjust treatment and constant attempts at strong-arming them into submission. Some families even succeeded in keeping their deeds in their possession and maintaining their businesses. After frustrating the Occupation's harassment efforts, were tempted with financial persuasions by the Occupying Authority to sell their shops and evacuate. New techniques emerge alongside tried and true methods of pressuring the remaining Inside-Palestinians to migrate. Even the smallest and oldest shops or houses and the properties located in Yafa's poorest areas were subject to over-the-top offers to sell. The primary goal of these merchants is to displace the rest of Palestinian Yafawians and possess their lands.

After the 1948 war, the Occupying Authority declared the establishment of a democratic and modern state, thus beginning a manipulative
marketing strategy of forging an image contrary to its coercive military
rule and its racist policies against the Palestinian people. Therefore, due
to these new strategic dimensions, the Occupying Authority understood
the importance of keeping quiet and downplaying human rights violations
by its forces, particularly regarding the recent massacres committed previous to and during the 1948 war. The Occupying Authority's strategies
for garnering the support of the international community are numerous.
Key to the occupier's agenda has been repressing knowledge of atrocities
committed by security forces, settlers, and militias in carrying out the ethnic cleansing of the Palestinian people and the continued looting and
settling of their land. This strategy was possible and effective up until the
second half of the twentieth century, but with the advent of new technol-
ogies facilitating the instant transmission of information and images, this
strategy became untenable. In an attempt to maintain the image of a new
peaceful, democratic state, the Occupying Authority began to harass and
imprison activists who tried to document its injustices. This sparked a
wave of violations against activists and journalists, still ongoing today.

The Inside-Palestinians were subject to displacement before, during,
and after the war. Prior to the establishment of its new state, the Occupying Authority enacted methods of ethnic cleansing to fulfill their Zionist
project.

Following the declaration of its new state, the Occupying Authority
added several new methods in order to continue its ethnic cleansing,
through rampant arrests, convictions, and imprisonment, often without
proper sentencing.

In Jinan Bastaki's work *Legacy of the 1951 Refugee Convention*, published in 2017, she illustrates how the "1951 Convention" on the Status of
Refugees was adopted by the United Nations to regulate the displacement
of refugees who find themselves exiled from their country of nationality
for any of the following five reasons: race, religion, nationality, membership
of a particular social group, or political opinion. Palestinians have fallen

victim to various types of forced migration since 1948, both from their country of origin, as well as from various host countries. The Occupying Authority does not recognize the Palestinian right of return, ultimately preventing the majority of displaced Palestinians from ever returning to their homeland. Palestinians, for the most part, have been left unprotected in their host countries; thus, have found additional hurdles seeking asylum in third states that are party to the UN 1951 Convention.[15]

Due to the difficult circumstances of Palestinian refugees, the United Nations introduced a new body, UNRWA; The United Nations Relief and Works Agency for Palestine Refugees in the Near East. The humanitarian organization operates based on the United Nations Charter and according to its legal framework and humanitarian principles of neutrality, impartiality, independence, and humanity. UNRWA's definition of the Palestinian refugee is "persons whose normal place of residence was Palestine during the period 1 June 1946 to 15 May 1948, who lost both their homes and means of livelihood as a result of the 1948 war." It is evident from this definition that not all Palestinian refugees were able to register- they had to demonstrate that they had lost both their homes and their means of livelihood due to the war. Founded in 1949, UNRWA's narrow mandate was temporary and assumed that refugees would soon be repatriated or resettled.

Primarily, before the creation of UNRWA, and in an effort to re-patriate some of the refugees back to Palestine, the UN passed the General Assembly Resolution 194, which articulates that refugees wishing to return to their homes and live in peace with their neighbors should be permitted to do so at the earliest date. Simultaneously, on April 27th, 1949, the UN created the UN Conciliation Commission for Palestine (UNCCP) to facilitate the repatriation, resettlement, and economic and social rehabilitation of the refugees, and the payment of compensation. Later, on December 8th, 1949, the UN created UNRWA to carry out its programs of direct relief and works to prevent starvation, distress, and to further conditions of peace and stability among the Palestinian refugees.

UNRWA was mandated by the UN General Assembly to meet the basic needs of Palestinian refugees that resulted from their plight. The agency provides Palestinian refugees with assistance, protection, and services such as education, healthcare, relief, and social services, camp infrastructure, microfinance, and emergency assistance in their host countries. Yet, the plight of Palestinian refugees is a political matter, and finding a just and lasting solution does not fall under the agency's responsibilities and it is not in fact a part of UNRWA's mandate.

Consequently, through the UNCCP, the UN offered to repatriate 100,000 Palestinian refugees, only 10% of the total population of Palestinian refugees. Thus, the Arab nations rejected the proposal on the grounds that all Palestinians deserved to return, and the occupying entity was rescinded from the whole proposal. Due to this impasse, the functions of the UNCCP became limited to collecting and maintaining refugee property deeds, a mission nonetheless vital to Palestinians today.

During his term, former US President Donald Trump launched an attack on UNRWA, announcing the withdrawal of US funding from UNRWA and from the formal peace process in its accepted, customary form. UNRWA's budget cut resulted in many school closures, freezing secular education for 500,000 Palestinian students. The operating UNRWA budget typically provides all kinds of medical and social services, providing basic levels of dignified living standards to the three million refugees benefiting from its mandate, who have been rendered stateless. Following Trump's decision, Palestinians formerly benefitting from the UNRWA program are forced to fend for themselves in an environment hostile to their very existence. In parallel, the Occupying Authority took advantage of Trump's support, emboldening illegal settlements and occupative policies. For various reasons, the Occupying Authority succeeds in evading most of the international community's attempts to hold it accountable for its illegal practices. The waves of Palestinian displacement continued after 1948 from the homeland, as well as from their host countries, despite feeble UN attempts at protecting the refugees.

Prior to the official failure of the United Nations' agencies in repatriating refugees to their homeland, and prior to frustrating the General Assembly's 194 Resolution, a few Palestinians were able to return to Palestine on the basis of the United Nations' Family Unification Law, which is part of UNRWA's humanitarian principles that facilitated the reunification of family members. According to Satel, Sha'aban Balha, a known historian and documentarian in Yafa, was expelled from Yafa, but was able to return as a result of the United Nations' efforts. Also, Mr. Balha's extensive knowledge of Yafa and the families that lived and owned properties and businesses there stemmed from his personal relations. He is aware of the locations and addresses of many Yafawian families' houses, lands, and orchards and he remained capable of tracing their locations even after many of them were demolished. Moreover, Mr. Balha can pinpoint and document the history of Yafa's main landmarks and spot them on the city's map; as well as being able to spot the villages that used to exist as satellites of Yafa before they were erased by the occupation. He left records that include significant information about Yafa's Old Town, its port, and the production and export of oranges and other citrus fruits. He also documented the illegal process by the British administration that allowed visitors to enter the country through Yafa's port on visit visas, facilitating their residency after the expiration of their visas. These illegal immigrants became the first settlers who took over Palestinian homes and properties.

The Abolishment of Yafa

Yafa's abolishment was part of a series of policies of erasure by the Occupying Authority which abruptly halted Palestinian development. The Occupying Authority's strategy of turning the major city of Yafa into a mere extension of Tel Aviv was to stunt the growth and development of the major Palestinian city. In 2009, the municipality of Tel Aviv hired a committee to prepare for the celebration of the centenary of Tel Aviv's establishment. The municipality allocated a big budget for the celebration and a special committee was assigned to prepare for a huge celebration. The committee invited musical performers and several writers and professors to deliver their speeches at this celebration, especially history professors, to focus on points requested by the authority. The Yafawians could see the fireworks in Tel Aviv's sky and they could hear people cheering, laughing, and singing. The people in Tel Aviv were celebrating their city, which Zionist leaders established a hundred years ago, while the people of Yafa silently lamented the erasure of their city.

Although Yafa was the economic and cultural capital of Palestine prior to 1948 and was generally regarded as Palestine's most modern and progressive city, the Zionist leaders' goal was to dim the lights on Yafa and its Palestinian Arab population and create their own modern city through the construction of Tel Aviv. In 1909, and prior to the declaration of the Balfour Promise, the Zionist leaders were confident of the execution of their occupative project in Palestine. Under the auspices of British colonialism, widespread in the Arab region and the main supporter of the Zionist project, Zionist leaders embarked on their project confidently. According to Mark LeVine, an American professor at the University of

California, Irvine, the Zionist idea was calling for a discursive, and ultimately physical, erasure of the Palestinian Arab population in the
surroundings of the new city. As a result, they demolished, and then wiped
off several towns, villages, and areas around Yafa and confiscated their
lands to build Tel Aviv in its place.

Yafa's northern villages were completely wiped off the map for the
same purpose. The project of the new city continued to expand throughout the years, which required the erasure of other areas from Yafa's
suburbs during the British Mandate period, including Sheikh Munis,
Jammaseen, Sumeel, and Jareesheh, which all disappeared. Hence, Tel
Aviv was established and expanded on the ruins of Palestinians and their
towns and villages.

Tel Aviv was created to be the country's developed economic, political,
and cultural center; a standard that the new city has maintained through
the years. Today, Tel Aviv is still the home of the wealthiest Jews in the
country, whose businesses kept the city affluent and developing. In 1950,
the Occupying Authority officially announced the annexation of Yafa to
Tel Aviv, calling a curtain on Yafa's cultural prominence and ushering in
a new era of extensive official campaigns of subjugation against its remaining indigenous inhabitants. Yafa was reduced to a suburb of Tel Aviv,
and all of its affairs put under the management of Tel Aviv's municipality.
Today, the country's map shows Tel Aviv in the place of Yafa, while Yafa
has been entirely erased off the map.

Following the 1948 war, in spite of the huge numbers of expelled Yafawians and to the dismay of the Occupying Authority, the remaining
families in Yafa still composed about one-third of Yafa's population. But,
after the annexation of Yafa into Tel Aviv, the Occupying Authority pursued the British colonial policy of gentrification, which, in this case, was
executed through the merging of two cities in order to mix their population and reduce the percentage of the unfavored ethnicity.

Accordingly, after the merge, the Palestinian population was dis-
solved into the larger percentage of Tel Aviv's Jewish population, which
reduced it to 2.8 percent. The Occupying Authority accomplished its

goal of reframing Palestinians as a minority living in the metropolitan area of Tel Aviv.

Similarly, according to LeVine, M. (2005)[16], Chomsky, N. and Pappe, I. (2015), and Pappe, I. (2006) this shrinking phenomenon was also applied to Yafa's neighborhoods. Prior to the occupation, Yafa consisted of twelve neighborhoods, all of which were bombed and destroyed to evict and displace their inhabitants. Today, only two and a half neighborhoods remain. The neighborhoods that remain have been subjected to an extensive Judaization policy by the Occupying Authority, a blanket policy applied to erase Palestinian identity wherever it persists and amounting to the purposeful transfer of a Jewish population to these cities and villages, to amass a majority Jewish population. There are several cities that have been subjected to Judaization, such as Haifa, Acre, Lod, and Ramleh.[17]

Satel (2018) states that the twenty residential units in Yafa that are known as the "Dokume" are a clear example of the Judaization of the city. These units were constructed right after the Nakba, exclusively for Jewish tenants, in order to Judaize Yafa. The "Dokume" was one of the earliest projects in Yafa post-1948, stealthily and gradually built on confiscated lands during the early stages of the occupation. The Yafawians learned that the Occupying Authority started its construction projects, after every wave of land confiscation, which is followed by the arrival of new waves of settlers housed in the newly developed residential units.

An objective behind the policy of gentrification was to merge or mix the percentages of Palestinian population, which were considered relatively high in certain cities, with the populations that were composed of an amalgamation of different nationalities. Primarily, those newcomers that were transformed in high percentages into the country were invited on a religious basis with the purpose of changing the demographics of Palestinian cities. Thus, the Occupying Authority had achieved its goal of minimizing the Palestinian population in the occupied cities, rendering them small minorities to facilitate marginalizing them, and practicing further encroachments on their rights. Paradoxically, though, regardless of any number or intensification of encroachments or violations by the Occupying Authority, it always seems to escape judgment, able to push through policies that amount to war crimes, such as those mentioned above. Moreover, it gets away with repeating those crimes that are reflected in its policies, strategies, and practices, such as hiding or fabricating historical facts, looting more Palestinian lands, and practicing more Judaization; not only on the Palestinians' history, culture, and identity, but also on their cities.

The endless attempts of Judaization are reflected in the early teams that were hired by the Occupying Authority to constantly open archaeological excavation sites in search of ancient relics pertaining to any Israelite presence in Yafa. As confirmed by Satel, who said that "the people of Yafa had never forgotten the teams of archaeologists that were hired by the Occupying Authority to search for any ancient relics or evidence that can be used as an indication for any ancient religious or other evidence to prove that the Israelite tribes had any way of life in Yafa, but all the excavation results were negative."

As mentioned previously, the politicization of geography and history is apparent every time historical data is used to serve political interests. Likewise, the proliferation of some religious information lacks studied historical data. As theologist Thomas Thompson states in *The Mythic Past*, the non-authenticated archaeological information is used as a loophole for some politicians for diverting peoples' attention toward certain directions for serving one or more political interests. Thompson separates between the ancient history of the Israelite tribes that is written today from the Bible's history, as he says, "Neither the ancient history of Judah, which historians write today should be the Bible's history... Nor is the history of Israel in the region of southern Syria the history of Eretz Israel, as called in several texts of the Bible." He confirms that Israel's ancient history is only a very limited part of the history of this greater region. And, he asserts, the incidents of its ancient history took place during the ninth and eighth centuries BC and involved only the region of the central highlands north of Jerusalem and south of the Jezreel valley.

Accordingly, not finding that evidence did not enable the Occupying Authority to accomplish its goal and made it difficult to politicize history in favor of its occupative project. When no artifacts were found in Yafa and the Occupying Authority could not have any evidence to prove its claim for an ancient existence in the city of Yafa, the Occupying Authority accelerated the annexation of Yafa into Tel Aviv, which ended Yafa's independence and turned it into a mere supplementary annexed area in the city of Tel Aviv.

Dictatorship Paradigm Under Military Rule

The suffering imposed on Yafawians in the aftermath of the 1948 war was a direct result of policies enacted by the occupying forces as living standards rapidly deteriorated and Palestinian rights were diminished. Indeed, each newfangled policy imposed by the Occupying Authority was forged to impair the Inside-Palestinians further. Likewise, the imposition of military rule on civilians, including families and children, weakened the Yafawians and added to their suffering. The Occupation Authority corrupted their lives, confiscated their lands, and forced them to live in strange and unfamiliar circumstances. As for the military rule, it confined them to live in an area that was made to be their prison. The conditions of the Yafawians continued to worsen with the worsening situation in Yafa. Especially, when Yafa lost its independence.

Under the Occupying Authority's military rule, the Yafawians lived confined and overcrowded. They were not allowed to live anywhere outside the zones prescribed by the occupation, which were under its full control. The Yafawians lived suffocated by restrictions imposed by the military rule. The lack of freedom in movement, for instance, prevented them from responding to their families' needs, including the ability to exit the assigned area to buy food and other necessities. To emphasize this humiliation, the occupying forces surrounded this area with a barbed-wire fence and made entering or exiting from it subject to permits that must be issued by the Occupation Authority's military.

According to Yafawians who lived through this experience, the occupying forces were adamant to see the Inside-Palestinians suffering the life of a ghetto, as many had been living previously in their European home countries. Thus, they established these assigned living areas for the Palestinians and aptly referred to them "ghettoes." The occupying forces did not only make the Palestinians' assigned living areas similar to the ghettoes they were forced into in Europe, even more unlivable as the occupying forces imposed a kind of military rule. Military rule had a perceptible effect on the lives of the Yafawians, who lived in dread over their lives and futures.[18]

The most famous ghetto after the occupation was the Ajami Ghetto in Yafa. Although the Occupying Authority succeeded in holding European countries responsible for the atrocities of the Holocaust and demanded compensation by compelling these countries to pay huge financial reimbursements, it nonetheless caused endless suffering to all Palestinians due to its atrocities, ethnic cleansing, and occupation. Although the Palestinians had nothing to do with the Holocaust, the Occupying Authority made them pay an extremely high price.

On May 13, 1948, after a consistent campaign weakening Palestinians through the aforementioned methods of oppression and restrictions, Mikhael Bin Jal, the military governor of Yafa, drafted what he called the "Military Statement" and called on a group of Yafa's headmen to surrender by signing it. Jal was also a member of the Haganah organization, which was known as the "Occupiers of Yafa." The military governor announced his "Military Statement" to the public and published its details in *Hartz* Newspaper. The job was assigned to journalist Shimon Samet, who wrote an article that can only be deemed offensive to every Yafawian. Samet focused on phrases and terms in which he described Yafawians as the defeated, overcome, and compliant people. Also, in his article, which many Yafawians still recall, military rule was announced, placing Yafawians under its strict control starting from June 11, 1948. The article goes into the invasive and inhumane details of the Military Statement. However, the Yafawians that had managed to remain in Yafa believed that not all was lost, because, in spite of all the practiced pressures, restrictions, and punishments against them, they were still living in their city, refusing to leave. The following are some of Bin Jal's Military Statement's most important points as stated in *Yafa; Fi Thilal Al Nakba* by Satel (2018) paraphrased and translated:

> *The Shooting on any Jewish entity or resistance against any Haganah member will be considered a violation and constitutes grounds for shooting back;*
>
> *All Palestinians are prohibited from carrying or keeping weapons of any kind. Weapons must be collected and taken to a designated area to be handed over to a Haganah representative. Any Palestinian who is caught with a weapon will be subject to severe punishment;*
>
> *All Palestinian men should gather in the "Ghetto" area, across from the seashore, to give their detailed information to the organization's representative to be included in the census and identifications. Those caught outside the designated area of the "Ghetto" will be punished severely unless they have permission;*
>
> *Each individual Palestinian will be issued an ID card, except those mentioned in item 5,*
>
> *Any Palestinian who threatens the security of any military groups will be interrogated and arrested based on military rules, and the Arab headmen must attend the investigation and must provide the military officer information about those who are under investigation;*
>
> *All military areas that are outside military rule are prohibited areas; only certain people are allowed to wander there;*
>
> *Palestinian individuals are not permitted to leave the areas of military rule without being issued permission to exit; similarly, Yafawian family members who live outside Yafa and want to visit their families in Yafa must first be issued an entry and exit permission to allow them entrance and exit to and from Yafa.*

> *Public institutions, public records, and public information are*
> *protected by the army. Palestinian individuals are not*
> *allowed to access any public information except*
> *with permission issued by the Military Governor;*
> *Palestinians will live in the "Ghetto" area and they will be*
> *monitored by a superintendent who will be appointed to*
> *oversee peoples' conduct, maintain order, and supervise their*
> *compliance to the above-mentioned regulations;*
> *The management of Yafa and all its affairs will be handled by*
> *Tel Aviv's Municipality;*

The articles of the Military Statement were not in place to maintain order and protect peoples' security but to humiliate and degrade one group of people in society and maintain their oppression through the occupation. Unambiguously, the Military Statement's articles that were formed against the most vulnerable, oppressed, unarmed, and occupied civilian group in society were merely another discriminative tool used by the Occupying Authority and its forces to keep the Palestinians overwhelmed by the occupation (Saltel, A. 2018 p.39–40)

Several war crimes and atrocities were documented and reported to the Red Cross. For instance, many of the rape crimes that were committed by the Zionist gang members were reported to the Red Cross, who investigated and confirmed them in special reports. The Red Cross held the Occupying Authority's soldiers responsible for these crimes. Many documented crimes talk about the soldiers that attacked families with girls, killed their parents in front of them, and then raped them. As stated by Ilan Pappe in his book The *Ethnic Cleansing of Palestine*, many of these crimes were reported to Ben Gurion. For example, he received a letter from one of the officers by the name of Chesek, stating that a group of soldiers broke into a house of a Palestinian family, killed the father, injured the mother, and raped the daughter (Pappe, p. 237). Yet no consequences were ever reported to have been instated.

The duration of direct military rule over Yafa did not last the way it did in the northern Palestinian cities, where most Palestinians clustered, composing the highest percentages of the internally displaced Palestinian population. This northern area includes the Jaleel area and the Northern Triangle cities, towns, and villages. The Yafawians claim that the end of Yafa's military rule was brought about to facilitate Yafa's annexation to Tel Aviv, admit thousands of new settlers to enter the country from Yafa's port, help many of them to settle in Yafa, and then, to commence the implementation of Judaization, a process which continues until the present..

All the same, until today, in broad daylight, the Inside-Palestinians who live under the occupation are surrounded by barbed wire. Daily, Palestinians today confront fully armed soldiers at checkpoints and all over the Occupied Territories. These soldiers' job is to hinder the mobility of the Palestinians, whether they are employees who need to go to work, kids walking to their schools, sick or elderly in need of treatment, or pregnant women whose babies are due.

All mobility is in the hands of the Occupation Authority. At the checkpoints, Palestinians experience humiliation and offensive treatment. Many mothers have given birth on the streets at different checkpoints, and many sick perish due to being unable to access treatment on the other side of the checkpoints.

Such control over the mobility of Palestinians plays out not simply to restrict their freedoms, but as the explicit, senseless murder of civilians in broad daylight. Such occurrences are endless, despite their unreasonable and unjustified details, these crimes remain impervious to accountability.

Demographic Replacements

Demographic change occurs when a population transitions through transmigrating from one country to another. Currently, demographic change by transmigration usually occurs for various socioeconomic reasons. However, the waves of movement into Palestine were purely for political reasons, for the formation of a Jewish, Zionist state in the land of Palestine. The leaders of the Zionist movement encouraged waves of immigrants to enter Palestine to alter the original demographics of the country in their favor. The permanent waves of transitional immigrants to Palestine have endured to serve the interests of the occupiers. For instance, since the beginning of the occupation of Palestine, the Occupying Authority has been challenged by the rapid growth in the population of the Inside-Palestinians, which sways the authority to keep motivating new waves of settlers to immigrate to the occupied territories, in an effort to maintain its sociopolitical goals by assuring demographics remain within its schemed percentages.

As published in the Journal of International Affairs article titled *The Politics of Demography in the Israeli-Palestinian Conflict,* demographics have been a major political issue for the Occupying Authority.[19] Subsequent to its occupation, the Occupying Authority realized an increase in the Palestinian population; therefore, it is in constant fear of being outnumbered by Palestinian Arabs. For reasons consistent with Palestinian Liberation Organization studies, such as the rising percentage of fertility among Palestinian women that reached about 8.3 births per woman, coupled with consecutive census results for the occupied territories in which the Palestinian population has reached 6.41 million

Palestinians versus 6.5 million for the Jewish population, this is a legitimate concern for the Occupying Authority. In spite of the occupying forces' various elimination methods against Palestinians from unjust treatments, torturing in its jails, to homicide, along with the ongoing transitioning of new settlers to enhance the numbers of its population; it is still expected in the near future for the population of the occupied territories to offset or exceed this small difference between the Palestinian and Jewish populations.

The above article mentioned a Haifa University geography professor, Arnon Soffer, and commented on his words during one of his interviews in which he spoke of the demographic changes. He claimed that the Occupying Authority's right-wing politicians, who call for one undivided Jewish state, have been striving to make the Palestinians of the occupied territories a small minority, so they often make up populations' percentages and birth rates to prove there are fewer Palestinians in the occupied territories than people claim. Furthermore, the Occupying Authority encourages the fanaticism of these politicians and adopts their falsified statistics. Soffer criticized this approach, saying that the right-wing politicians "invent things to enable the annexation of the occupied territories."

Years ahead of their occupation and before the end of the 1800s, the religious passions of thousands of European, Russian, and Eastern Jews were inflamed by the Zionist leaders' inspirations about migrating to Palestine. Many of the first settlers entered the country illegally. The new waves of settlers that arrived in 1918 were brought with the intention to settle in the city of Jerusalem, and had been sent there with the explicit aim of changing Jerusalem's demographics. Thus, whether these waves of newcomers came illegally into the country, entered as immigrants, or on visit visas, they all entered Palestine with one goal, which is to impose a change in its demographics.

The goal of the Zionist leaders was to create a population base to begin implementing their occupation project, which Great Britain had promised them. They needed a foundation to rely their claims on and to emphasize assertions, such as claiming that Palestine was a "land without a people," or, encouraging the narrative of the divine "chosen ones." Hence, Zionist leaders changed the country's demographics and built a population base that enabled them to establish a strong pretext for the execution of their project in Palestine.

The initial transmigration of the Jewish population to Palestine took place in stages. The first stage lasted from 1882 until 1891; the second stage lasted from 1904 until 1918 and continued after the British Mandate over Palestine. These two stages raised the number of new settlers in Palestine to 85,000. Many of these newcomers entered the country from Yafa's port and they ended up staying in Yafa. These transmigrations were executed under British cover, support, and financing. These newcomers were welcomed by the Palestinian people, who at the beginning were unaware that they were not visitors, but immigrants entering Palestine as part of a new occupative plan.

According to the *Jewish Immigration to Historical Palestine* article published on the Canadian for Justice and Peace in the Middle East (CJPME) site, dated November 2013, Palestine's Jewish population numbered about 25,000 and had been deeply rooted there for several generations.[20] But, after the first stage of transmigrations, between 20,000 to 30,000 settlers entered Palestine, most of whom were Russian Jews who escaped from Czarist Russia. During the second stage, more Russians escaped and entered to establish themselves there; they numbered between 35,000 to 40,000, most of these settlers participated in the establishment of Tel Aviv. In the 1920s, more Jewish immigrants arrived in Palestine, around 35,000, from Poland and the Balkans. And after WWI, the transmigrations to Palestine were stimulated once again, and by 1931, the Jewish population in Palestine reached 174,600, forming 17 percent of the general population of Palestine. However, between 1932 and 1939, there was another stage of transmigrations to Palestine, which raised the numbers of the Jewish population to 247,000; 46 percent of these newcomers came from Europe. After 1948, the Occupying Authority opened a wider door to admit larger transmigrations from all over the world.

According to the CJPME, the British were in favor of the establishment of a Jewish national home in Palestine. The British administration
was very lenient with the settlers, and the newcomers took advantage
of this lenience. When the waves of these newcomers increased, they
provoked the Palestinians, who started demonstrating against the British
administration, which put the British administration in political crossfire
and obliged it to levy some regulations on immigration. Yet, the newcomers resorted to circumvention and thwarted the rules of the
administration and its effort to regulate immigration, using methods such
as faking university registries at the Hebrew University in Jerusalem, or
falsifying marriage intentions. Many entered on tourist visas and never
left.

It was a group of these newcomers who established the very first local
Jewish newspaper, written in English and Hebrew, *Hartz*. It was in *Hartz*
that the commencement of the occupation of Palestine was published
through the pronouncement of a Jewish homeland. After the initiation
of the occupation, the Occupying Authority used the new newspaper to
circulate news about imposing its iron fist on the indigenous population.
To spread the news and keep the leaders of other Palestinian cities in-
timidated, the Occupying Authority published its imposed military rule
treaty, which it forced the leaders of Yafa to sign, and published it in the
Hartz newspaper.

Topographic Transformation

The topography of any city consists not only of its natural and urban features, but its history, its peoples' language, belief system, and culture — all factors which compose their identity. Hence, topography includes both tangible and intangible features. These features within Palestinian cities were targeted by the Occupying Authority, which has remained adamant about changing or obliterating them. Consequently, Palestinian cities are not only subject to the repetitive topographical changes that arise from physical, chemical, or biological processes that cause natural topographic transformations, but also, to intentional social topographic transformations through the interference of the Occupying Authority in these occupied Palestinian cities. Their original historical, geographical, and cultural features are subject to complete alteration in order to create topographical changes that serve the occupier's occupative and political interests.

Even now, with our increased capabilities of interconnectedness and exchange of ideas, culture, and interaction across the globe, the Inside-Palestinians are subjected to increasing limitations, separation, marginalization, and confinements behind barbed-wire, partitions, checkpoints, and cement walls that are fixed to separate Palestinians from each other, from their lands, homes, resources and general accessibility.

In 1949, the Occupying Authority signed an Armistice agreement with its neighboring countries under the guise of ending the atrocities of the 1948 war, and enforcing new borders with Egypt, Syria, Lebanon, and Jordan; this line is known as the Green Line.

The Occupying Authority started building an illegal cement wall along the newly minted Green Line - a construction which violated international law. Afterward, in 2003 it submitted an advisory to the United Nations General Assembly for resuming its construction of the cement wall, stating that it will "partially" follow the Green Line. But, the construction of this illegal barrier exceeded far beyond the Green Line. The International Court of Justice (ICJ) found that the separation Wall violated international law and should be torn down. This Judgement is referred to in the United Nations General Assembly Resolution 66/225 of December 22nd, 2011. However, it remained non-binding and the building of the wall was extended over more Palestinian lands, sometimes running right through private lands, separating families, and annexing homes and fields.

Similarly, other topographic changes in the Palestinian cities began early after their occupation, including the demolition of homes and other buildings, the removal of landmarks, restrictions on the usage of the Arabic language, and the falsification of historical information. Many of these endeavors target the histories of these cities that goes back to thousands of years BC.

The Occupying Authority is still constantly in search of justifications and loopholes to be able to meet the extreme demands of its most conservative far-right politicians and proponents without triggering human rights organizations or international law. Many of these prove difficult to legitimize, for example, the repeated demands to demolish the Aqsa Mosque, and the failure in discovering Israelite archeological traces in some Palestinian cities. The Occupying Authority's constant processes of topographic mutation also seeks to justify certain claims that work to legitimize the establishment of a Jewish state in Palestine, such as in the "Land Without a People" narrative, which was adopted by the Occupying Authority as a strategy to affect and control Western public opinion. The success of the proliferation of this narrative is limited, however, as it was easily refuted by numerous Western and Jewish politicians, scholars, and historians, such as Avi Shlaim, Ilan Pappé, Noam Chomsky, and many others.

Since 1898, the founding father of political Zionism, Theodor Herzl, became acquainted with Palestine and its original people and encouraged the migration to Palestine and the change in its demographics. It was well known by the Zionist leaders and their movement that Palestine was a developed country and was always inhabited by its Arab Palestinian people. The history of Palestine did not halt with the departure of any conquerors. The Zionist leaders were granted the opportunity to execute their occupative project and come to Palestine as its twentieth-century invaders. But, the indigenous population's oral and written history form plausible accounts that can be compared by historians with the land's archeological findings.

Accordingly, since the occupation, the topographies of the Palestinian cities have been subject to various changes that are damaging; there is an ongoing confiscation of property, destruction of landmarks, demolition of homes, uprooting of trees and entire orchards, the destruction of cemeteries, diverting of roads and avenues, transforming the function of existing buildings, overriding of the Arabic language, and imposing barriers to keep Palestinians confined and separated behind checkpoints, barbed-wires, and illegal cement walls.

The municipality that owned Yafa's confiscated lands and properties constructed new houses on the ruins of the Palestinians' houses. These constructions and projects were not only to fill Palestinian neighborhoods but also to convey an extremely discriminative message against them. The Andrew Mida project, for example, it is a modern and luxurious neighborhood that was established on the ruins of a Palestinian neighborhood. It was built for wealthy Jewish immigrants. Its inhabitants enjoy living a high level of luxury in the gated community. There is a gardening space located between the living structures and the fence that contains a variety of beautiful trees, shrubs, and flowers, which are also planted in the outside area around the fence to enlarge the zone of isolation.

Yafa's streets and neighborhoods were given foreign names, while their original Arabic names were wiped away. This strategy was adopted from the British colonization, whose administration during mandate times implemented its mixing or gentrification of cities policy. For instance, the name Al-Ajami Street, was changed into street number 60; it was not even given a name, but it became, as the people of the land have become, just a number. Other street names were altered, for example, King Faisal Street was changed to "Yahuda Himit Street," Jamal Pasha Street is called today "Shadrot Yirushalem Street," Al-Hilweh Street became "Yaft Street," Abdel-Raouf Bitar Street became "Shabti Israel Street," and Dajani Street became "Dr. Arlekh Street."

The names of neighborhoods were also changed. For instance, the neighborhood of Jabalya was changed to Bijan Tamar. Even the name of Yafa became Yafo. The Tel Aviv municipality was responsible for erasing the Arabic language from all the shop banners, street signs, and advertisements around the city in an attempt to negate Yafa's Arabic identity. The municipality also prohibited the printing presses from printing new Arabic banners or signs, and levied an extra tax on shops with existing ones printed in Arabic.

The Municipality of Tel Aviv assigned a spot on Yafa's seashore for Tel Aviv's city waste. A twelve-meter hill across from the Ajami neighborhood was constructed to replace 3,200 demolished Palestinian homes. Nothing was spared from these crimes, not even the dead were left to rest in graveyards. With the usual disrespect to everything Palestinian, the occupying forces aggressively exhumed several graveyards, disinterred corpses, and threw them away. The Yafawians have submitted many complaints demanding the authority stop grave exhumation, but the infringements on their graveyards continued and their demands were ignored. Similarly, all other complaints that the Yafawians filed demanding the municipality stop its infringements on their mosques and sacred places, such as the transformation of Hasan Bay Mosque into a pig farm. The Occupying authority also ignored the complaints against changing street names, the removal of Arab inhabitants from the old town, the conversion of Al-Manshiyeh neighborhood into a park, and many other transformations.

The Yafawians deem their minaret, which can be vividly seen from a distance, as one Yafa's important features. Thus, silencing their main city's minaret was a social, cultural, and religious encroachment. They miss listening to the beautiful sound of the "Athan," or call for prayer

The village of Sheikh Munis is among the examples of the erasure of entire villages. The Palestinian inhabitants of Sheikh Munis were evicted from their village by force and their lands and properties were confiscated. Only 2.5 kilometers from the Mediterranean Sea, the village was located in northern Yafa, nine kilometers from the city center. Its proximity to Al-Auja River gave its lands a particular fertility, color, and ambiance. The entire village of Sheikh Munis was confiscated by the occupying forces, who established in its place a Hebrew university. A place of higher learning which excluded Palestinian students, who remained banned from higher education for decades. The Hebrew university became today's Tel Aviv University. Yet, the Palestinians, who were born in Yafa's Sheikh Munis no longer have a birthplace. As Satel sadly commented, "the Yafawians who were born and lived in the obliterated villages, their place of birth has vanished." His mother, for example, who was born in Jareesheh, saw her birthplace erased while during her lifetime.

The development built over the ruins of Yafa, now called Hertzia, extends over an area of 26 square km West of Tel Aviv. It has become one of the most elegant and richest neighborhoods of the country, with embassies and residences of foreign diplomats and businessmen. This city that was founded in 1924 by wealthy Jewish immigrants has today a population of 87,000 people. This area, once one of the most familiar areas to Yafawians, has become entirely unrecognizable.

Despite the thoroughness of these crimes of ethnic cleansing, many Inside-Palestinians have remained adamant about staying in their cities. The aforementioned mutations of Palestinian cities were attempts to disturb the Palestinians' sense of familiarity with their hometowns, and turn them into strangers in their own cities, as well as deplete their efforts to stay resistant. Nonetheless, these ongoing criminal strategies were unable to accomplish the occupation's goal of erasing Palestinian existence and forcing the majority to leave. The Occupying Authority has committed and continues to commit countless crimes in the hopes of ending Palestinian presence and forcing the majority of those living inside to leave. Nevertheless, the Palestinians understood the intent, which only encouraged their endurance and resistance, and have been standing firmly in the face of violence for over seventy-two years, insisting on staying in their homeland, and refusing further displacement.

Multiple Damages by Manifolded Occupative Policies

The demographic and topographic transformations enacted in Palestine are war crimes that involve destroying civilian properties, pillaging, looting, and illegal evictions, amongst other violations of international humanitarian law. Yet, the Occupying Authority has continued to commit these crimes unabated, in parallel with their supplementary occupative policies, for over more than seventy-two years. The iterations of these crimes have created imminent perils on the Arab Palestinian identity of the people, their cities, history, culture, and language.

These crimes of erasure entail the extermination of the Palestinian people on ethnic, racial, and religious bases from society, whether by committing massacres against them, or by expulsion, displacement, discrimination, or marginalization. In addition, these crimes work to rid of all that constitutes the Palestinian Arab identity through fabrications, obliterations, demolitions, and other illegal actions, in order to transform the identity of the Palestinian cities into the identity of their occupier.

Irrefutably, the Occupying Authority's persistence in enacting rules and forging policies that lead to illicit outcomes against one ethnicity within society is an outright violation of international laws. These processes of ethnic cleansing and the transformation of topography follow complex and long-term measures; thus, in order to be achieved, they depend on committing other crimes. As the prelude to the events of the

Nakba and the occupation of Palestine, the demographic transformation, for instance, has been associated with the commitment of incessant crucial crimes against the Palestinian people and their properties, such as demolishing huge numbers of Palestinians' houses. In turn, this crime has also led to several other crimes, such as the displacement of thousands of families, confiscation of their lands and other properties and businesses, extraction of trees, and orchards. In its pursuit of ethnic cleansing, for example, according to Wikipedia, the Occupying Authority "had razed 49,532 Palestinian structures as of 2019."

All the policies and punitive measures of the Occupying Authority are designed to meet the requirements of the completion of its current occupying plans; their fulfillment expedites the accomplishment of its primary goal of a Jewish state. The Occupying Authority has been working on reinforcing its occupation on Palestinian lands since 1948. After annihilating the Inside-Palestinians, and expelling and displacing thousands of others, the Occupying Authority continued increasing its use of military force and arbitrary policies against the Palestinians who stayed in Palestine in order to complete its occupation over their lands.

Jerusalem and the Myth of the Temple

In 970 BC, the Canaanite King Sadiq was the first to call the city of Jerusalem by its name. Then, King David established the Kingdom of Judah, which remained a united kingdom under his rule between 1011–971 BC. King David and his son, King Solomon, were prophets in the monotheistic religions, and according to what was mentioned in David's Psalms, he intended to build a temple for worshiping, but did not live to achieve his wish. Thus, his son, Prophet Solomon implemented his father's wish and ordered the construction of a luxurious temple surrounded by a spacious courtyard to accommodate huge crowds of worshippers. According to the biblical psalms, this temple turned the city into a holy city. But, after the death of King Solomon, conflict arose among his people, which ended their unity and led to the separation of the disputants into a northern kingdom. The people of the two opposing kingdoms continued to battle until they both became weak and unable to deter foreign invasions.

As a result, in 587 BC, both kingdoms were defeated by the Babylonians under the leadership of Nebuchadnezzar, who occupied Jerusalem and demolished the temple. Nebuchadnezzar took the people of the two defeated kingdoms to Babylon. Fifty years later, the Persians defeated the Babylonians and King Koresh allowed the Jews to return to the Land of Canaan and build a new temple in 537 BC. Yet, in 333 BC, the land was conquered again by Alexander the Great, who defeated the Persians and put Canaan under his rule. Consequently, everything in Canaan, including the character of its cities, was imbued with the Greek civilization, the temple was demolished, and the Jews were deprived of practicing their religion openly. They did not regain their right to practice their religion until the Maccabean revolution took place in 160 BC. Afterward, they succeeded in regaining their right to worship.

In 63 BC, the Romans conquered and defeated the Greeks. The Roman leader Herodias ruled the Land of Canaan, and during his reign, Jesus Christ (PBUH) was born. In 70 AC, the Jews rebelled against the Romans. After many Romans were killed on the streets, the Roman Emperor sent an army under the leadership of King Titus, who besieged the city of Jerusalem and succeeded in ending the genocide that was being committed on the streets against the Romans. Moreover, the Romans burned the temple and banned the Jews from entering Jerusalem. During Hadrian rule, the name of the city was changed to Eliya, and the country's name was enshrined as Palestine. Throughout the period of Roman rule, especially during the reign of King Constantine, the identity of Jerusalem changed from Jewish to Christian due to a mix of exile and conversions. Consistent with the orders of the King's mother, Helena, churches were erected all over Palestine. She wanted a church everywhere that Jesus (PBUH) had been, and gave orders for building the Church of the Holy Sepulcher in Jerusalem; hence, these changes inspired huge numbers of pilgrims to make yearly pilgrimages to Jerusalem.

Once more, in the seventh century, the Persians conquered Palestine. The Jews took advantage of this incident and collaborated with the Persians, so they could enter Palestine again. In 614 AC, the Persians allowed the Jews to go back to Palestine. When the Jews returned to Palestine, they slaughtered thousands of Christians. Fifteen years later, the Roman army conquered Palestine under the leadership of Hercules. They won the battle against the Persians and retrieved the Romans' rule in Palestine.

Afterward, the advent of Islam ushered in a whole new era and its beliefs and culture pervaded the entire region. In 636 AC, the Caliph Omar Ibn Al-Khattab arrived in Palestine to define the location for building the Aqsa Mosque in the location of where Prophet Mohammad's (PBUH) Night Journey and Ascension into Heaven occurred. The establishment of the Aqsa Mosque remained minimal, until it was enlarged later in 709 AC. Nonetheless, in 691 AC, under the dynasty of the Umayyad State, the Caliph Abdul Malik ibn Marwan established the Mosque of the Dome of the Rock and wanted it to be characterized with a golden color dome, due to its sacred position as the third holiest mosque in the world for Muslims. Since then, Jerusalem, the Holy Land and the city of peace, opened its gates to the Jewish, Christian, and Muslim worshippers, until the Crusades, European military expeditions that were organized to invade Palestine and recover the Holy Land from Muslims throughout the 11th, 12th, and 13th centuries.

This struggle over Jerusalem that reinstated violence between Christians and Muslims was first recouped after the triumph of the Muslim leader Salah Al-Deen in the battle of Hattin in 1187. After his death, however, the Crusades resumed and regained the city of Jerusalem. In 1244 AC, the Muslims recouped Jerusalem all over again under the leadership of the Muslim leader Nijm Al-Deen Ayoub. Later in history, Palestine was conquered by the Tatars, who were defeated during the Mamluk Dynasty and under the leadership of King Peppers in 1260 AC, in the battle of Ain Jalut against the Mongol Empire. Successively, Palestine and Jerusalem were put under Egypt's rule until the end of the Mamluk era and the advent of the Ottoman Empire, which was known for its ferocity and sufficiency in wars. The Ottomans ruled the region for four hundred years from 1517 until World War One.

Following the year 1922, the League of Nations granted Great Britain the right to put Palestine under its mandate. Meanwhile, the British administration in Palestine gave the Zionist movement a green light to begin the implementation of its occupying project in Palestine. The British collaborated with the Zionist movement and facilitated the occupying process; starting with the admittance of thousands of illegal immigrants from all over the world into Palestine, passing through the famous promise that the British made to grant Palestine to the Zionist movement to establish a Jewish state within Palestinian territory. The Mandate ended with a major deception on the part of the British administration, when it silently withdrew, leaving many thousands of Palestinian families to face the fully armed and well trained Zionist fighters, most of whom entered the country for the purpose of occupying it and displacing them, though the mandate agreement stated otherwise.

The occupying forces then divided Jerusalem into East and West, and evicted the Palestinians from the Western section after it confiscated their lands and other properties. After the Naksa war in 1967, the occupying forces also extracted the Eastern section of Jerusalem from its Palestinian residents, demolished a large neighborhood to build settlements in its place, and brought in a new wave of immigrants to replace the expelled Palestinians. This is one of the most common occupative strategies, bolstered by the attempt to implant Jewish historical roots in Palestine, principally in the West Bank and Eastern Jerusalem, to claim a longer and older historical existence in Palestine that exceeds the Palestinians' existence in their country by establishing settlements in sensitive areas; particularly, in Jerusalem. In October of 2022 Estrin, Daniel, a PNR representative reported from Jerusalem the establishment of three big settlement projects that are being advanced around Jerusalem. One of them is Givat Hamatos. In spite of the objections of European diplomats to the project of building settlements in the occupied Palestinian territories, the Occupying Authority's expropriation of Palestinians' lands resumes; especially, in very sensitive Palestinian areas.[21]

The results of the unremitting search for any monuments or ruins did not serve the interests of the Occupying Authority, and its Archaeologists long excavation did no find a physical evidence; thus, deeds were fabricated to allege legitimacy. Ingrid Jaradat, from the US Campaign for Palestinian Rights highlights Israel's colonization of Jerusalem and attempts to Judaize the city of Jerusalem by displacing its native Palestinian population and creating a Jewish demographic majority through dispossession and other policies that lead to the impoverishment of thousands of Palestinians. The Occupying Authority is planning laws that legalize the expropriation of large amount of Palestinian land allocating them for public needs. Also, it continues denying the rights of Palestinians to obtain permits to build houses or repair any of their properties to push them out of Jerusalem. As a result, to these policies, almost 200,000 Israeli settlers live on stolen Palestinian land in East Jerusalem, while the apartheid wall separates about 140,000 Palestinians in Jerusalem neighborhoods like Kufr Aqab, Qalandiya, and Abu Dis, from the rest of the city. Palestinian Jerusalemites are also denied access to basic infrastructure: only 59 percent of the 324,000 Palestinians in Jerusalem are connected to the city's official water grid (Webinar on Colonization and Gentrification).[22]

Gentrification is an old colonial strategy, employed by colonial powers to serve their political interests. Currently, the Occupying Authority applies this strategy in the construction of huge settlements, most of which contain over a thousand residential units to accommodate residents of certain religious, ethnic, and ideological beliefs; in order to change not only the demographics of Jerusalem and other Palestinian cities in occupied territories but also to alter the Palestinian cities' culture and identity.

This occupative strategy is being employed currently in Eastern Jerusalem, where the settlers are backed by the occupying army, police, and the extreme right-wing in the Occupying Authority's government. Settlers have gathered in East Jerusalem in large numbers, making claims around several Palestinian homes, working to expel their residents. This is part of a larger plan to merge the Eastern section of Jerusalem to its Western section by expelling large numbers of Palestinians and marginalizing the remaining minority. What is most significant is that by occupying East Jerusalem, the Occupying Authority will automatically gain control over the entrances to the Islamic and Christian Quarters in Jerusalem. Therefore, the consequences of the Occupying Authority's illegitimate and unjust policies and strategies go beyond violating the religious rights of the Palestinian Muslims and Christians in the Holy City, to violating the religious rights of millions of Muslims and Christians around the world by controlling their access to their sacred sites.

For example, controlling the highly contested Sheikh Jarrah neighborhood means controlling the internal passages and corridors leading to Al-Aqsa Mosque. This gives settlers the ability to roam freely in the courtyards of Al-Aqsa Mosque and resume the excavations they started years ago in search of the temple, which they still claim is buried beneath Al-Aqsa Mosque. Although this belief was refuted and proven wrong by many theologists and archaeologists, such as Thomas Thomson, who insists that this belief is based on misinterpretations of some biblical psalms. Yet on these grounds, the Occupying Authority's most fanatical and extremist religious groups demand their government expedite their promise of establishing Temple Mount, which they hope, one day, will replace the Al-Aqsa Mosque.

The Occupying Authority is not required by any law to present real evidence for any of its claims. So, it continues making all kinds of occupative policies, and regardless of the means it uses to implement its policies, it remains above the law. These infringements on justice, with the continuous oppression against Palestinians and the serious violation of their human rights, are happening under the eyes and ears of western superpowers and Arab countries that support the occupation, or at the very least, reject deterring it.

PART THREE

PART THREE

Looted Freedoms &
Violated Human Rights

*"Since when have you compelled people to enslavement, when
their mothers birthed them free."*

— OMAR BIN AL-KHATTAB

The 1948 occupiers' invasion of Palestine put an end to the liberty and
security of the Palestinian people, and violated their rights with excessive
use of power, torture, and ethnic cleansing. The occupiers implemented
policies based on violence, discrimination, and infringements of the Palestinians' freedoms and human rights, which continue until today. As a
result, thousands of Inside-Palestinians are arrested and imprisoned
without trial. Others suffer the direct and indirect consequences of ethnic cleansing through forced evictions, demolitions, and illegal
confiscation of their properties. They find themselves having to live with
various combinations of oppression, persecution, and displacement. The
Inside-Palestinians suffer numerous coercive and discriminative policies
and punitive measures that are imposed on them daily by the Occupying
Authority.

The lives and futures of all Palestinians are heavily affected by the
loss of their homeland, whether they remain living under the occupation,
ended up scattered in countries around the world, or suffered an arduous
life in a refugee camp.

The calamity of the occupation leads to losing one's homeland, freedoms, and identity. Confining people in restricted areas behind cement walls, barbed wires, or military checkpoints prevents them from their right to move freely, is a violation of international law.

Many Palestinian people are prevented from reaching surrounding areas around their neighborhoods. They are compelled to abide by the occupying forces' restrictions or face punishment by fully armed soldiers, who are capable of ending their lives in an instant. This forces the Palestinians from different towns and villages to live prolonged and indefinite detentions behind restrictions that are built around their designated areas. In addition, these confinement policies contribute to the impoverishment of Palestinian families and augment their economic deterioration. Inside-Palestinians' economic and political degradation was fully supported by other colonial powers to preserve the Occupying Authority.

Although various populations in Western countries have experienced civil wars to achieve their emancipation and to end tyranny, injustice, and inequality in their societies, their countries and governments nonetheless support the occupation of Palestine, and other violations of freedom and human rights in the Middle East. France, in August 1789, defined basic human rights in the second Article of the French Natural Human Rights, in its French Declaration of the Rights of Man and the Citizen as follows: "The end in view of every political association is the preservation of the natural and imprescriptible Rights of Man; these rights are liberty, property, security, and resistance to oppression." Yet, it looted and violated the freedoms and the basic human rights of millions in the Middle East and North Africa, most notably its occupation of Algeria, where countless Algerians were killed resisting French oppression.

Subsequently, as published by the Human Rights Resource Center at the University of Minnesota; edited by Nancy Flowers, there are thirty universal articles of human rights and freedoms. According to the Universal Declaration of Human Rights, and most countries' constitutions, all human beings must be granted the following rights and freedoms:

ARTICLE 1   *Right to Equality*

ARTICLE 2   *Freedom from Discrimination*

ARTICLE 3   *Right to Life, Liberty, Personal security*

ARTICLE 4   *Freedom from Slavery*

ARTICLE 5   *Freedom from Torture and Degrading Treatment*

ARTICLE 6   *Right to Recognition as a Person Before the Law*

ARTICLE 7   *Right to Equality Before the Law*

ARTICLE 8   *Right to Remedy by Competent Tribunal*

ARTICLE 9   *Freedom from Arbitrary Arrest and Exile*

ARTICLE 10   *Right to Fair Public Hearing*

ARTICLE 11   *Right to be Considered Innocent until Proven Guilty*

ARTICLE 12   *Freedom from Interference with Privacy, Family, Home, and Correspondence*

ARTICLE 13   *Right to Free Movement in and out of the Country*

ARTICLE 14   *Right to Asylum in other Countries from Persecution*

ARTICLE 15   *Right to Nationality and the Freedom to Change it*

ARTICLE 16   *Right to Marriage and Family*

ARTICLE 17   *Right to Own Property*

ARTICLE 18   *Freedom of Belief and Religion*

ARTICLE 19   *Freedom of Opinion and Information*

ARTICLE 20   *Right to Peaceful Assembly and Association*

ARTICLE 21   *Right to Participate in Government and in Free Elections*

ARTICLE 22   *Right to Social Security*

ARTICLE 23   *Right to Desirable Work and to Join Trade Unions*

ARTICLE 24   *Right to Rest and Leisure*

ARTICLE 25   *Right to Adequate Living Standard Personal Security*

ARTICLE 26   *Right to Education*

ARTICLE 27   *Right to Participate in the Cultural Life of Community*

ARTICLE 28   *Right to Social Order that Articulates this*
             Document
ARTICLE 29   *Community Duty Essential to Free and Full*
             Development
ARTICLE 30   *Freedom from State or Personal Interference in the*
             above Rights

The first article of the Declaration of Universal Human rights and Freedoms states that all human beings have the right to equality. But, social equality, or egalitarianism, is a concept that is absent under any occupation. There is no equal treatment under the government of the Occupying Authority; it treats all Palestinians as second-class citizens, and all its institutions, courts, public and private organizations, and proponents discriminate against the Palestinian people. The settlers are allowed to use weapons against Palestinians and inflict bodily harm, sometimes resulting in death. They are also allowed to sabotage Palestinian orchards, depriving them of harvesting their olives; the only source of income for many rural communities.

In fact, the system on which this occupying entity is based promotes inequality by pronouncing that not all humans are equal in fundamental worth or moral status. An article published in Haaretz on November 5, 2018, under the title of *Everyone Knows Settlers Cut Down Palestinian Olive Trees,* exposes through photographs, maps, and videos examples of this crime in one area in the occupied territory in October 2018. The settlers who dwell at the far outposts in the northern West Bank attack Palestinian farmers, steal their produce, and destroy their olive trees. Additional related articles by Haaretz reveal the loss of Palestinians' trees during other periods, confirming the destruction of hundreds of Palestinians' olive and citrus trees by groups of settlers, either violently or through water deprivation.

Settlers have been destroying Palestinian groves and depriving them of access to springs, other water resources, and irrigation processes, in an attempt to stop the growth of Palestinian crops. These methods have left many Palestinian families impoverished. For instance, Burin, a town located near Nablus city, was dependent on a particular spring as its main source of irrigation. This spring was turned into a site for religious ritual baths exclusively for the settlers' use. It was plundered from the Palestinians, who became prohibited from accessing the spring or using its water. As a result, the trees in Burin's groves dried up and died. As usual, the settlers were not held responsible for damaging Burin's groves. Neither the police nor the courts are known to deter or constrain the settlers' illegal practices against Palestinians. On the contrary, for the past seven decades, the Occupying Authority has been encouraging these constant crimes against anything Palestinian, be it people, buildings, or trees. Thus, settlers are allowed to commit any crime that causes loss or damage to Palestinians and their properties.

In addition, the right to freedom from discrimination does not exist under this occupative system, where discrimination is embedded. Exhausting and disuniting the occupied population hinges on the application of extra racist and discriminative methods among the occupied people themselves as a means to create divisions, factions, and avoid the possibility of unity amongst the Palestinian people. Thus, the Occupying Authority does not only use racism and discrimination to create severe distinctions between people of the same society, comprised of Arab Palestinians and the Jewish population, but it also applies discriminative methods at all levels on the basis of religion, race, and ethnicity.

According to Jablonski, an anthropologist and paleontologist at Pennsylvania State University, "Race is understood by most people as a mixture of physical, behavioral, and cultural attributes. While ethnicity recognizes differences between people mostly based on language and shared culture." Thus, race is perceived as inherent in our biology, which transmits from one generation to another, but ethnicity is acquired based on shared factors such as location and culture.

There is a dual practice for the government of the Occupying Authority the emanates from the tension between the Jewish-Zionist and Western-secular images of the state. Sasson-Levy, Orna (2013) argues that "While Israel's Jewish discourse supposedly negates intra-Jewish ethnic conflicts, the Western ideal identifies Ashkenazim with the state, thus solidifying their power and preserving their privileged status.[23] The Occupying Authority considers its white Ashkenazi European Jews a superior social stratum in its Jewish society. This idea of the superiority of one race over other races in the body of the same population is based on the eighteenth-century definition and consideration of race, which was perceived and used by the colonial powers of that time as a separation tool between humans. In retrospect, colonial European countries espoused this idea as a principle to highlight and separate societies' certain biological traits of people. This principle guided the crafting of colonial policies that classified people in terms of their geographical locations and skin color. Given such flawed principles, the foundation of racism was officially established and fortified. All colonial European powers advocated this principle, which encouraged their armies to commit atrocities against indigenous populations based on classifying them as inferior. Likewise, those serious distinctions between people on bases of geographical locations and skin color became embedded in all the occupative policies and practices of the Occupying Authority, which, on the one hand, discriminates among the Jews themselves, as well as Jews and Arab Palestinians, and on the other hand, also discriminates between Palestinians on racial and religious grounds.

Palestinians neither have the right to equality, nor do they have freedom from discrimination. For instance, settlers are allowed to use abusive language and practice countless infringements, including murder, against unarmed Palestinians of all ages without any repercussions. This leniency on the part of the Occupying Authority leads to an increase in the severity and level of discrimination against Palestinians. For example, the Palestinians are tagged and referred to in derogatory terms such as the "foreign enemy," "fifth column," or "demographic dilemma." Accordingly, UN human rights experts expressed alarm at the rising rate of violence directed by Israeli settlers towards Palestinians in the occupied Palestinian territory.[24]

Above and beyond restricting the movements of Palestinians, the Occupying Authority hampers the choices, beliefs, lifestyles, and behaviors of all the Inside-Palestinians. Whether they are restricted by barbed-wires and checkpoints, segregated behind the high cement wall, or imprisoned behind bars, the constant constraints and inhibitions that are imposed on the motions, wishes, and actions of Inside-Palestinians take away their liberty, render them an oppressed people, and augment their sufferings.

Palestinians are also deprived of the freedoms that are stipulated in articles five to eleven in the above-mentioned law of the International Human Rights, such as the freedom from torture, degrading treatment, and due process rights. As confirmed by B'TSalem, the Israeli information Center for Human Rights in the Occupied Territories, there are thousands of Palestinians who are deprived of their right to trial and they suffer administrative detention and incarceration of unlawful restrictions. Through the long years of occupation thousands of Palestinian youths spent their lives imprisoned without charges or fair trials. Currently, the incarcerated Palestinians, both men and women have remained deprived of their rights of recognition and equality before the law, such as visitation rights, or the right to fair trials. Furthermore, they are often subject to cruel treatment or torture, regardless of gender, age, or health conditions. The courts of the Occupying Authority often fabricate reasons for illegal imprisonment and unlimited, or extended periods. There are countless cases for Palestinians who spent their lives behind bars and without charge, evidence, or due processes rights. Palestinians are often arrested for what are recorded as 'administrative reasons.' While the Occupying Authority's "Administrative Imprisonment" has no legal basis, it is employed as a cover for the illegal arrests and imprisonments of Palestinians. According to the Palestinian Society Prisoner's Club, there are currently 4,400 Palestinian prisoners, 70 of them are women, and 40 are children, most of whom have not been indicted.[25]

Often, an occupative policy or strategy violates more than one article of human rights, such as the policy of recruiting spies from among the

Palestinians, often young people. This occupative method violates not only the security of those spied upon but also the personal security of the youth recruited through threats, pressure, and exploitation of poverty. This sort of espionage is an enslaving of the youth; an abhorrent interference with the privacy of families in their homes, it restricts opinions and information, sows seeds of mistrust, damages the mental health of the recruit and interrupts their education, and imposes social underdevelopment by hindering the development of Palestinian communities and their cultural life. Therefore, the enforcement of espionage on the Palestinian youth and their communities is a violation of Article 30, which protects individual freedom from the interference of the state in personal matters.

In Yafa, for instance, the espionage phenomenon emerged early, soon after the occupation began, through the recruitment of spies to work in favor of the Occupying Authority and against their families and their people. The authority took advantage of the imposed financial hardships and blackmailed the youth into spying on their communities. These youth, being inexperienced, were often quickly revealed and ostracized from their families and their larger community as a result.

In response to this social and security scourge, the majority of Yafawians have remained watchful and careful in everything they say or do. The threat of espionage is a continued dilemma that afflicts Yafawians. It invades their privacy in their own homes, compromises their safety and security, and causes major distress. This phenomenon has increased the Yafawians' social underdevelopment, due to losing some of their Yafawian youth, who were meant to stay in schools and find regular jobs to help their families; yet, they were enslaved and put under extreme pressures and became fully controlled by the security apparatus," Satel writes.

This is an example of how the Occupying Authority uses direct and indirect methods to disenfranchise Palestinians. The recruited youth find themselves under severe pressure to deliver information about their people and if they do not, they are threatened and tortured. But, once the recruited spies leak information about one of their community members, the torture of this member begins.

Therefore, espionage from within Palestinian society is like a lesion in an organ of the body. It renders the Palestinian people more vulnerable, increases their insecurity, and rouses suspicion from within. While they are with or among their community members, they must remain alert and restrict their freedom of expression and opinions.

Another interrelated series of violations against the Palestinian population that occurs daily is the levying of restrictions on movement. These restrictions violate Articles 13 to 17 of the Universal Declaration of Human Rights as restricting peoples' movement impacts other daily activities and the accessibility to necessities. This includes daily obstruction on the movements of laborers, doctors, patients, teachers, students, and other social groups that need to run errands, respond to duties, or seek livelihoods. Fully armed occupying forces keep them waiting for hours at checkpoints. One intention behind these violating and often absurd checkpoints is to complicate the process of movement for Palestinians, making them undesirable and obstructing their mobility, accessibility, and the carrying out of their everyday lives. They hinder workers from reaching their workplaces on time, the pregnant and the sick from reaching hospitals, and children from attending school, just to make life more difficult.

According to the 2021 socioeconomic report by the United Nations Conference on Trade and Development (UNCTAD), The West Bank has been suffering since two decades a deteriorated economy that led to deepening poverty and increasing unemployment rates. The economic losses in the occupied territories are estimated by $57.7 billion, due to the closure policy and restrictions that were imposed by Israel after the outbreak of the second Palestinian Intifada (uprising) in September 2000. According to the UNCTAD report the imposed closure and restrictions on the Palestinian economy have lowered the West Bank's GDP per capita by 44% than its actual value, and the increased poverty rate would have been 12% instead of 35%.[26]

The right to return to one's country is guaranteed by the United Nations Universal Charter of Human Rights. Indeed, the right of return stems from the sanctity of private property, which does not expire in the case of occupation, state sovereignty, or the passage of time. The right to return to one's country is an individual right according to a number of legislations, and therefore, this right is not subject to delegation or representation, and it cannot be overridden or waived in any agreement or treaty.

Restricting the entrance to the 1948 territories and the ghettoization of Eastern Jerusalem are violations of Palestinians' right to adequate living. Additionally, the Occupying Authority is prone to sudden additions to its restrictions. For example, in 2009, it renewed the ban on West Bank Palestinians to prevent them from obtaining legal status in the 1948 occupied territories, including those whose spouses carry East Jerusalem identities. These restrictions violate marriage and family rights. For example, if the wife or the husband is a resident of Jerusalem, and the other is a resident of the West Bank, that means they carry different identity cards and are subject to different rules and restrictions. Before this rule took effect, these couples may have lived together in Jerusalem. After its implementation, married couples that hold different identity cards could no longer live together in Jerusalem. This brings about the unnecessary suffering of countless families.

The Occupying Authority also violates the rights of Palestinian refugees to their nationality. Since the 1948 war, it has constantly rejected Palestinian refugees' right to return to their original cities, towns, and villages in Palestine. It simply refuses to acknowledge this massive humanitarian issue caused by its aggression and occupation. This unwavering refusal includes the refugees' return to zones in the West Bank, which are classified as Palestinian territories.

The right of return is a collective right according to the right to self-determination, which the United Nations affirmed in 1974 in a statement that comprehensively describes Palestinian rights and refers to them as "inalienable rights," and therefore does not lapse in the event of a peace treaty. Of course, the Oslo Agreement of Principles has no legal value to deny "inalienable" rights. Therefore, the Occupying Authority's policies and measures of restricting Palestinians' freedoms are illegal, and represent major violations of internationally agreed human rights.

The nature of the Occupying Authority and its government are based on discrimination and social inequality. Under its governance, the naturalized Palestinians are not treated as citizens with full rights and are not granted the same political freedoms that the Jewish portion of the population enjoys. Also, the Inside-Palestinians who live in the 1948 territories are not privy to the socioeconomic advantages or benefits, or even access to natural resources, that settlers are granted. This occupying entity enacts all its occupative policies on discriminative foundations. Turning Palestinians into citizens of the Occupying Authority did not render them equal to the Jewish citizens. The Occupying Authority treats all Inside-Palestinians as occupied people, and they remain threatened by its occupative policies, such as demolition, confiscation, oppression, and the use of coercive power against them. The policies segregate the Inside-Palestinians and force them to live clustered in much smaller areas.

Since its establishment, the occupying entity on Palestinian land has practiced religious discrimination against Muslim and Christian Palestinians. It imposes restrictions that prevent them from practicing and attending prayers or masses in mosques or churches. For instance, through the period of military rule in Yafa, the mosques and churches were shut down, and Yafawians suffered from being denied permission to leave their neighborhood to attend prayer or mass.

A more recent example arises in Jerusalem, where Muslims between eighteen and fifty years of age are prohibited from practicing their religion in Al-Aqsa Mosque, under the pretext of "security." Likewise, many Christians who live in various Palestinian cities are blocked from reaching Jerusalem during pilgrimages and the Christmas season. If some families have members who live in the blocked zones, they are deprived of being together during Christmas.

Though the Occupying Authority has long acquainted itself with the Palestinians' Islamic culture, both its security forces as well as its settlers

continue to commit offensive physical, spiritual and sentimental infringements on the religious locations, practices, and values of the Palestinians.
These infringements are intended to cause deep emotional and spiritual
wounds. The perpetrators are aware of the value of purity to Muslims,
and they know about the profaning acts or factors; first, due to some
common beliefs between Judaism and Islam; second, due to their obtained
knowledge of nuanced intricacies of Palestinian culture. Yet, they continue desecrating and profaning mosques and places of worship. Actions
such as the confiscation and subsequent neglect of the Hasan Bey
Mosque, which led to becoming a site for illicit drug and sex trades, are
degrading to Palestinian religious and cultural beliefs.

Identity Obliteration

Obliteration, according to the Oxford Lexical Dictionary, is the deletion or erasure of something; to obliterate is to destroy, cancel, or make something invisible by hiding it or erasing it from being and mind. Obliteration was exercised during World War II by the armies of the Allies against the Axis countries, such as the obliteration of Japanese towns and cities by the US Air Corps. Equally, the Occupying Authority has been exercising this policy since the nascent days of its occupation of Palestine; it has been destroying the Palestinian cities' tangible landmarks and obliterating their original history, identity, and culture. By the same token, the Occupying Authority practiced its policy of obliteration and ethnic cleansing on the Palestinian people through several massacres against Palestinian villages, towns, and people who all vanished from the surface of the land. As a consequence, the implications of the obliteration policy go beyond their visible damages; they penetrate into the original people of the land, leaving behind permanent psychological and emotional damages.

It has become impossible to imagine Palestinian national identity without the Nakba, as it is equally impossible to separate it from the Arabic identity. The tragic Palestinian experience and its extension over seven decades did not cancel or detract from the Palestinian identity. Nor did it come at the expense of an Arab identity, which is the foundation of Palestinian identity that is well-established in the Arabic language, history, culture, and thought. It can be said, then, that Palestinian identity is a strong, stable identity that cannot be easily obliterated.

The implementation of the identity obliteration policy is responsible for all the intentional alterations of the original Arabic names and histories

of Palestinians' streets, neighborhoods, and landmarks, and for the elimination of property deeds by forging and fabricating documents; sometimes
after concealing information and facts, other times by obliterating them.
Through this continuous implementation, the Occupying Authority in
Jerusalem and elsewhere in the occupied territories attempts to conceal
evidence that connects the Palestinian people with their properties,
whether those properties are lands, homes, orchards, or shops. Generally
speaking, identity refers to the totality of how a person connects to their
roots, culture, language, and history, which informs their own perspectives
on an individual and collective future. Therefore, the ability to know, un-
derstand, realize and manifest one's identity is undoubtedly valuable for
an individual and a community. Being acquainted with the factors of one's
identity provides them with foundational knowledge about the conditions,
placements, and possibilities related to their past, present and future.

In general, Palestinian identity possesses a particular stance - one
that is consistently informed by its state of occupation, which influences
their capabilities, feelings, thought patterns, and behaviors. The occupation and its constant oppression and aggressions have formed the basis
of the Palestinians' identity for the past seven decades, which is now in-
extricably tied to notions of resistance.

The identity of resistance expresses the Palestinians' rejection of the
state of occupation. Inherent in it is a promise to continue the struggle
for their lands and their freedoms. The common identity of resistance in
Palestinians at home and across the world also reinforces Palestinian
unity, illustrates a rejection of the fragmentation of the Palestinian people,
the displacement of Palestinians, and the persistent enactment of policies
that refuse the return of the Palestinian refugees to their lands. This key
component of resistance across Palestinian identity is a constant challenge
to the Occupying Authority's attempt to relinquish its responsibility and
accountability to the refugee populations that live stateless for generations
due to their policies.

Despite being separated, confined, or far-flung, there are common
foundations to the Palestinian identity that can be represented in a tri-

angle, each side of which indicates a basic pillar of identity: the unity of the people, the demand for liberation, and the call for the establishment of an independent Palestinian state on Palestinian land. These common factors that resonate in most Palestinians from all walks of life and all over the world work to invigorate the Palestinian cause. This threatens the Occupying Authority, and pushes them to repeated endeavors to weaken or obliterate the pillars of Palestinian identity that maintain and reinforce their sense of belonging to their land, history, and culture. In light of this, Palestinians consider the clarity and strength of their identity as critical factors for their unity. A well-defined identity improves self-understanding and provides displaced populations with internal integration. These pillars of identity provide Inside-Palestinians with higher thresholds of resistance, and endurance while facing the daily challenges that are imposed on them by the Occupying Authority, or, if they are refugees or in the diaspora, keeps them from feeling removed and distant from the cause. A powerful aspect of Palestinian identity stems from the firm belief in their right to live on their land, and from their adherence to their right to return to their country. The identity of Palestinians, who have been struggling to survive, remains influenced by their enduring struggle, which is understood as an existential struggle.

Enraged efforts by the Occupying Authority to shake and weaken Palestinian identity have continued until today. However, Inside-Palestinians understood the purpose of these endeavors and knew that they could only be challenged with steadfastness. Thus, the very presence of Inside-Palestinians, whether in their hometowns or displaced elsewhere in the occupied territories, is in itself a threat to the occupation and its goals. By remaining in the lands of Palestine, they are confronting the Occupying Authority's policies and strategies of displacement and attempts at obliteration. Irrevocably, Inside-Palestinians have proven their ability to confront the Occupying Authority. The Inside-Palestinians' identity of resistance has not diminished across generations. On the contrary, the rising generations reinforce the resistance and find new ways to carry it forth.

On the other hand, the Zionist identity has remained rooted in its religious foundations since it came to being in 1896, when Theodor Herzl's proposal for a modern solution for the Jewish problem was published in the "Judenstaat" in February of that year. Based on religious aspirations, the Zionist identity was adopted by fanatic groups in the early stages of the occupation of Palestine. It then became incorporated into the political fabric of the newly established state and its Occupying Authority. The Zionist identity was at first imposed on certain factions in the population, and quickly became a major ideology within the state. Yet, until today, the Occupying Authority claims that the identity of its state is secular and democratic.

The Zionist identity reflects in some ways Machiavellian political philosophy and ideology. On a basis of the "end justifies the means," the Occupying Authority and its proponents commit their crimes and violations against the Palestinian people. Despite the obvious imbalance of power, the Occupying Authority has established itself as the only maker, implementer, and actor in this struggle towards the creation of a Jewish state, and considers its struggle with them an existential struggle.

Since the conflict began on the land of Palestine, Palestinians have suffered from the biases of the international community, particularly powerful western nations with a personal interest in maintaining the superiority of the Occupying Authority.

The Occupying Authority that seized over 80 percent of Palestinian land continues its crimes without interruption or accountability. Also, it routinely rejects or infringes on agreements, concessions, arrangements, or negotiations. It often thwarts formal negotiations with Palestinian representatives, especially those that present a two-state solution; sometimes by outright refusal, and other times by evading solutions and conclusions. Thus, the Occupying Authority is intentionally obstructing the establishment of a Palestinian state on any part of the land. The Occupier will continue to provoke and prolong conflict, obstruct resolution, and expand territory, because they will accept nothing less than the complete occupation of all Palestinian lands.

The Intentional Deterioration of the Palestinian Educational System

The Palestinian people have always appreciated the value of education; this was indicated in the prevalence of schools in Palestinian cities, towns, and most villages. Palestinians were conscious of the relationship between education and development, so the literacy and educational rates were quite high until they became occupied and lost their freedom. The Occupying Authority since the beginning of its occupation imposed several restrictions on the Palestinian schools' curricula to defect the Palestinian educational system, curtail the education of Palestinian younger generations, and restrain their socioeconomic development.

The Palestinian's high regard for education is depicted in their societal achievements on various levels, including numerous urbanized coastal and non-coastal Palestinian cities, as well as in different cultural and socioeconomic developments. The Palestinians' ancient civilizations and rich history have also had a great impact on their current education values, as well as management skills. Through the years, Palestinians have been steadfast in learning about their land, soil, and abundant natural resources, and have ascertained beneficial usage of their resources, facilitated by the country's advantageous geographical location, which renders it extremely fertile. Despite the regressions of the different transitional periods during their history, the Palestinian appreciation for education, liberalization, and progression was always evident, illustrated in their capabilities of survival and coping with difficult circumstances. Throughout history, Palestine has experienced more periods of liberty, prosperity, and development than periods of mandate, servitude, occupation, and underdevelopment. The multifaceted skills of the Palestinians have always been evident in their handicrafts, production, urbanization, and advanced agribusiness and agronomy, which the occupation has been attempting to incapacitate and seize for their own since it established itself on their lands.

Since 1948, the Occupying Authority made concerted efforts to destroy the Palestinian educational system to instill and perpetuate illiteracy and a lack of education, which brings about a variety of endemic deteriorations. In a study on ignorance, conducted by Shepherd and Kay (2011), it was deduced that feeling unknowledgeable isolates people from their surroundings. This has a psychological effect on an individual, which, in turn, manifests in a reluctance to learn.[27] Thus, in tandem with dismantling the educational system, the Occupying Authority worked diligently to block facts and information relevant to the history of Palestine. Historical facts that challenge the Zionist narrative were erased from academic books, newspapers, and other secondary sources. Historical information, including interpretations of certain biblical Psalms, were manipulated and disseminated, swaying the public opinion of the international Jewish community, as well as Western powers, in their favor. Accordingly, the Occupying Authority maintained these claims within its territories and beyond to keep its occupation grounded, facts about Palestine and its people, and its propaganda and claims accepted and institutionalized.

The Occupying Authority insisted on fragmenting and destroying the educational system and making it difficult for the rising generations of Palestinians to gain a proper education. Their method to purposely spread ignorance among Palestinians was not only to make them feel unknowledgeable, and thus, insecure, but also to keep them lagging behind their occupier counterparts as well as international standards. Ignorance is antithetical to progress. Thus, the leaders of the Occupying Authority were aspiring to achieve increased percentages of ignorance among younger Palestinians to increase their dependence and make them unable to verify information. Also, dependent and less educated populations may have more of a tendency to rely on fake news and believe the flagrant lies of authoritarian figures, which hampers motivation and causes severe societal deterioration.

As mentioned, each occupative policy results in a variety of detrimental outcomes. Destroying the education systems in Palestine not only increases illiteracy, ignorance, and basic levels of functioning, but also subsequently leads to higher poverty levels. The two lesions of ignorance and poverty combined in turn cause many other social and economic deteriorations that intensify the Palestinian population's socioeconomic underdevelopment, stunt their political capabilities, deepen their dependency on the occupying state, and essentially distance them from their freedom.

But propagating ignorance is not easy in a society that clings to the value of education and understands the relevance between education, independence, and liberty. The Occupying Authority and its forces have experienced the difficulties of subjugating the Palestinian people. In spite of all the occupative practices that have been causing severe damage to the Inside-Palestinians and their educational system, very few of their expectations were met. This authority may have achieved some of its goals and reaped the benefits that empower and lengthen its occupation, but it also learned that increasing its oppression leads to an increment in the Palestinians' steadfastness. The damages caused by the Occupying Authority will always remain limited, as long as Inside-Palestinians remain in their country.

Education empowers people with knowledge; it provides them with the necessary security and stamina to defend their freedom and rights. It allows them to maintain tolerance and restrain violence, and builds hope for the future. In 1948, Palestinians had confidence in their educational system. It is proven in UNDP indices and reports that there is a significantly high percentage for elementary education completion in 2003, yet a percentile regression for continued secondary and higher education (UNDP, 2003). According to the UNDP study on Arab human development in building knowledge society, the net enrollment ratio (%) in Palestine for primary education of both genders was 99.14; the highest in the Arab region, while in Egypt it was 92.32. According to the same report, it shows enrollment rates in the secondary education in Palestine have seen a huge drop to 76.90 and a greater regression of 25.95 for tertiary education. For the sake of comparison, these percentages have risen in Egypt for both educational levels to 79.03 for the secondary and 39.00 for tertiary.[28] This regression in the Palestinian ratios signifies the influence of the Occupying Authority on Palestinians and the impact of its imposed policies and restrictions that are levied on them to deepen their poverty, hinder their socioeconomic development, and keep them under its occupation.

In parallel with the violent activities of the Nakba, the Occupying Authority immediately and strictly targeted the Palestinian education system. First, it shut down many schools in cities, towns, and villages, bringing the number to a minimum, leaving them overcrowded and overwhelmed with students. Next, Palestinian teachers, many of whom were exiled during the Nakba, were replaced with immigrants. The Occupying Authority then transformed the curricula at all levels, changing the system and manipulating the syllabus to suit their interests. Moreover, with many Palestinian families falling into poverty, children were taken out of school and put to work.

The demolishing of schools was comparable to the demolishing of houses. While some schools were turned into barracks and military bases, others remained open, but only for the children of the settlers and new immigrants. Due to the segregation policy, the Occupying Authority did not allow Palestinian children to go back to their schools. For instance, in Yafa, the Arab Orthodox College on Hraish Road, which is located close to the Ajami neighborhood, was turned into a military base. The schools that remained open were subject to a segregation policy and rejected Palestinian children, except for the Hasan Arafah School, as it was located in the jurisdiction of the military rule. Many campuses were turned into service buildings. The Occupying Authority opened centers for distributing services to its new immigrants in the Palestinian schools and changed their tasks and nature. Then, the Occupying Authority eventually allowed some Arabic schools to reopen and receive students; however, it kept them underfunded, overcrowded, and restricted their curricula (Satel, A 2018).

Another occupative method employed to corrupt the Palestinian education system targeted the teaching process. Subsequent to expelling many Palestinian teachers from their country during the 1948 war, the Occupying Authority allowed only a few elementary and middle schools to reopen under their rule, but refused to hire Palestinians to fill the teaching vacancies in their schools. It restricted these vacancies exclusively to its new immigrants, some of whom arrived from neighboring Arab countries, with no regard to qualifications. As a result, the Palestinian schools' new teachers lacked knowledge, teaching techniques, and essential skills, causing untold damage to both the teaching and learning process.

As a matter of fact, since the commencement of the Jewish movement into Palestine, Zionist leaders used various incentives to persuade hundreds of thousands of immigrants from their countries of origin around the world to sail to Palestine. First, these leaders built their argument on religious grounds, asking Jewish populations around the world to migrate to the land they claimed was granted to them by God. They also encouraged migration by offering materialistic gains - a new, national homeland that would be exclusively theirs to develop. Many Jewish immigrants were enticed with financial security, guaranteed work, or a bountiful life.

Based on these promises, it was important to the Occupying Authority to provide job opportunities for its new immigrants, place them on a payroll, and improve their living standards so that they would settle and remain. Naturally, these new immigrants were also employed to accomplish tasks that serve the Occupying Authority's interests. The new teachers facilitated the Occupying Authority's falsification of facts and information, dissemination of a certain ideology, and control over the youth.

According to many Inside-Palestinians who were school children in the early 1950s, the new teachers were not considered professional teachers. Rather than focusing on education, these teachers were often used as eyes and ears by the authorities, gathering information about the children's families. They were also employed to impose the occupation's ideologies, and to punish children who spoke against or challenged it. The new hires interfered in the curricula and made changes as required by the Occupying Authority. They monitored textbooks to prohibit repeating terms and ideas that were not approved by the authority and were not in favor of its occupation, including the term "occupation" or any terms that indicated the inhumane practices of the Occupying Authority or any of its forces. Their job was to nip the bud of ideas or practices that might lead the Palestinians to objection, opposition, insurgency, or revolution. Terms such as Arab nationalism, unity, victory, or steadfastness were immediately thwarted. Similarly, words such as Palestine, Palestinian people, or the history of Palestine also became taboo.

Likewise, the Occupying Authority mandated the new teachers to monitor the behavior of students on the anniversary of the 1948 war during the imposed celebrations, which all Palestinian schools are forced to hold annually. Every year, the students of each school must raise and salute the flag of the occupying state. Forcing an occupied population to celebrate the anniversary of their occupation and their Nakba is inhumane.

This policy of forcing Palestinian students to celebrate the anniversary that sparked their ongoing catastrophe only serves as a reminder to Palestine's future generations of the number of years they have lived suffering under occupation. The Occupying Authority may continue to force Palestinian students to celebrate its 'independence,' but in the minds of the students, they know these crimes of ethnic cleansing and plundering of lands cannot be called independence. Furthermore, the question remains; independence from whom?

Such policies of obliteration are deeply-rooted and expansive. The Occupying Authority takes pains to render such language obscure in an effort to wipe them from the past and future memories of generations of Palestinians. The Occupying Authority also exerted effort to stagnate the curricula of Math and Science by obstructing the application of updates in the textbooks and syllabuses. Over the years, this resulted in a lag and deficiency in the two subjects, which hindered students' entry into university in fields that required an evolved and current understanding of math and science. This was especially debilitating in the decades before the advent of the internet, as Palestinian students were kept from learning about the accelerating technological and scientific developments occurring in the world. This policy stunted the growth of occupations such as doctors and engineers within the Palestinian population. By thwarting the math and science curricula, the Occupying Authority deepened the destitution of Inside-Palestinians, made it more difficult for their communities and societies to thrive, and kept them further detached from the outside world. This strategy prohibits future Palestinian generations from being connected with world advancements to halt any developmental endeavors by them and to aggravate their present political and socioeconomic marginalization.

The closure of high schools was another manner of attacking the Palestinian education system. In Yafa, for instance, the Occupying Authority shut down all the city's high schools immediately after occupying Yafa in 1948 and for nineteen years. Throughout these years, the Yafawian youth and the youth of other Palestinian-occupied cities were deprived of continuing their education and disqualified them from pursuing university studies. The closing of high schools for nearly two decades had a detrimental impact on Palestinian communities for long after. In 1967, after the defeat of the Arab armies in the Six-Day War, the Inside-Palestinians managed to reobtain the basic right of continuing their education.

In mid-1967, after Egyptian President Gamal Abdel-Nasser blockaded the Gulf of Aqaba, the Occupying Authority launched preemptive airstrikes against the Jordanian, Egyptian, and Syrian armies, and led bloody battles on the ground. The war ended in a massive Arab defeat after Jordan lost the West Bank, Egypt lost the Gaza Strip and the Sinai, and Syria lost the Golan Heights. Over 20,000 Arabs were killed in less than 144 hours in various battles during this brutal war. These enormous Arab losses occurred due to the vast difference between the armies of the two sides. The occupying army was supported by the US, Great Britain, and France, which granted them insurmountable advantages. Its army surpassed the other three armies in organization, military equipment, air force power, and access to accurate information about the confronting armies. Accordingly, these advantages rendered the occupying army far more efficient than the three Arab armies combined.

This war is known as the Six-Day War, or in Arabic, the Naksa—the "setback." It was indeed a setback for Palestinians and the Arab countries in the region; instead of ending the occupation the 1967 war led to its expansion. As a consequence, the occupation today extends to over more than 92% of Palestinian land, with ongoing confiscations, annexations, and settlements currently threatening the remaining 8%. Today, the Occupying Authority makes it very difficult for Palestinians from the West Bank and Gaza to enter the 1948 occupied territories. The 1967 war brought about big changes in the map of the Middle East. It led to a growth in the economy of the occupying state and provided it with more power and hegemony. It also imposed new public discourse that yielded the occupying state more power.

After its aggression on Egypt in 1956, the occupying state continued to consider that Egypt, along with Syria, represented a threat to its security. But, after the 1967 war and the seizure of large areas of Palestinian, Egyptian, and Syrian lands, the economy of the occupying state became unaffected by the old state of war; a new stage had commenced with bigger occupative plans and policies. Along with its developing economy, the Occupying Authority became focused on new policies such as land confiscation on larger scales, the establishment of settlements on the remaining Palestinian lands, the Judaization of Palestinian society, and mostly, on securing its acquired lands and taming its neighbors. Thus, the policy of closing Palestinian high schools was no longer important. The Occupying Authority was establishing itself as a new, progressive, democratic state, and could sacrifice the intensity of the Palestinians' demand for the schools to be reopened to keep the issue from resonating in the West.

A study on "Culture, Poverty, and Education by (Constance, Elam 2002) confirms the relevance between the two variables of poverty and education under specific cultures and socioeconomic situations. The study refers to a powerful statement made by a mountain woman who expressed her priorities saying "Livin's more important than schoolin'" This powerful statement condenses the complex socioeconomic situation into the priorities of mountain life.[29]

Living a mountain life could be considered difficult, where in many countries the inhabitants of such an environment could suffer plenty of difficulties and face many challenges to survive; thus, subsistence in such culture comes before education. Likewise, by comparing the hardships of a mountain life with the hardships of living under occupation we find that people who live under occupation face more difficult challenges and they go through more dangerous situations that constantly threaten their survival. Particularly, when the ruling authority does not treat them equally, deprives them from their basic human rights, and works on impoverishing them. In fact, living under occupation does not only impact peoples' choices, but also the availability of certain benefits or privileges to choose from. For instance, the absence of Yafa's secondary schools that remained closed for nineteen years by the Occupying Authority means that this benefit did not exist and was not available for people to choose it. Similarly, the Inside- Palestinians who prioritize education over subsistence find themselves in more difficult situations when their children's public schools do not provide their children with education, due to the flawed school curricula, or when the Occupying Authority uses these schools for espionage purposes. Therefore, living under the occupation remains the main coefficient factor that influences the Inside-Palestinians' culture and priorities.

Ignorance is a state brought about by a lack of education and knowledge which limits peoples' opportunities to fit several jobs that help people improve their social standing. Education, on the other hand, empowers people with skills and abilities and widens their opportunities to earn more and improve their living standards. Consequently, lack of education reflects on the general well-being of individuals, as well as on their society. Under the occupation, peoples' social, cultural, and economic developments lag behind and their poverty deepens, which in turn, due to the circumstances of the impoverished, gives birth to ignorance.

The Occupying Authority often precludes employers from hiring educated Palestinians into fruitful positions, and instead keeps them in low-wage jobs. These imposed financial difficulties hinder many Palestinians from continuing their education. Poverty forces families to pull their children out of schools and put them to work to help the family to survive, making child labor rampant. Such poverty appeared in Palestinian society during the Mandate years; yet, it did not become widespread except under the current occupation. This socioeconomic issue which victimized generations of children has continued from 1948 until our current time.

But despite the Occupying Authority's repeated, prolonged, deep, and evolving dedication to the obstruction of Palestinians' education, the Palestinian's tenacity continues to frustrate the carrying out of their goals.

Silent Ethnic Cleansing: Settlement & Judaization

The settlements are sprawling compounds and complexes established to accommodate huge numbers of settlers, whom the Occupying Authority invites from around the world into Palestine. Occupative policies such as the demolition of houses, confiscation of land, or eviction of families from their homes, often make way for the establishment of settlements. As has been made clear in previous chapters, Palestinians, whether Jews, Christians, or Muslims were living peacefully as one nation on their land with very little sectarianism or conflict among them until the Zionist project was implemented.

The Inside-Palestinians whose homes may have survived demolition incidents remain subject to eviction in favor of settlers at any time. Palestinians, like most Arabs, often lived in extended family homes, with generations living together. This means that before the occupation, many Palestinian families have been living in inherited houses for decades. The occupiers supposed they can change this fact, embezzle Palestinians' houses, and establish massive settlements to replace Palestinian homes and residential neighborhoods. They did this by promulgating historical and religious allegations claiming false ownership of Palestinians' houses and lands.

The suppositions of the Occupying Authority and its belief in being able to change facts emanate from the unlimited support that it receives from the world's superpowers, which enables and empowers the occupying entity's political claims, military capabilities, and economic life.

In lieu of such endorsement, primarily in the form of state-of-the-art weaponry and huge financial donations, the Occupying Authority perpetuates its oppression and its coercive powers against Palestinian civilians, including illegal crimes such as the annexation of Palestinians' homes and lands to establish additional settlements. Particularly prescient as well is the absence of legal accountability by the international community, which encourages the occupying entity to continue carrying out its crimes.

The Occupying Authority's settler policy leads to the displacement of the local population, which contradicts fundamental rules of international humanitarian law. According to the Statute of Settlement, Article 49 of the Fourth Geneva Convention states: "The Occupying Power shall not deport or transfer parts of its own civilian population into the territory it occupies." It also prohibits the "individual or mass forcible transfers, as well as deportations of protected persons from occupied territory."

The extensive appropriation of land and the appropriation and destruction of property required to build and expand settlements also breaches various other clauses of international humanitarian law. Under the Hague Regulations of 1907, the public property of the occupied population (such as lands, forests, and agricultural estates) is subject to the laws of usufruct; which, as stated in Wikipedia, usufruct according to civil law means a limited real right under mixed jurisdictions that unites two property interest of "usus" and "fructus." Usus is (use). It is the right to use and enjoy a thing possessed, directly and without altering it which means that an occupying state is temporary. Amnesty International published in Chapter three of one of its publication on the status of settlements under international law stating that the limitation of possessing any Palestinian property is derived from the core idea of the law and the notion that occupation is not permanent. In addition, in the same publication, the International Committee of the Red Cross asserts that the occupying power "has a duty to ensure the protection, security, and welfare of the people living under occupation and to guarantee that they can live as normal a life as possible, in accordance with their own laws, culture, and traditions."[30]

The Zionist leaders' plan to bring millions of illegal immigrants into Palestine works to constitute a nation of its proponents to replace the land's original inhabitants. The settlers were incentivized with the promise of fully furnished homes in thriving communities. Massive settlements were built on lands confiscated from Palestinians, after demolishing their homes.

Settlements are encircled with trees, flowers, and various plants that are irrigated with water stolen from the surrounding Palestinian towns and villages, which are left to suffer water scarcity. The construction of settlements remains the primary form of land theft. For instance, the two settlements in the city of Al Khalil, Kiryat Arba'ah and Abu Ghunaim Mount are expansive Occupying policies.

Presently, the occupying forces are still evacuating Palestinians from their homes by force of arms to build more settlements; as has been happening in the neighborhood of Sheikh Jarrah in East Jerusalem. In retrospect, during the first and second Oslo Accords, the United States and some Great Power European countries placed intense pressure on the Palestinians to sign a cession of 78 percent of their lands to the occupiers and accept only 22 percent of the total historical land of their country if they were to establish some semblance of an independent Palestinian state. This was a historic mistake on the Palestinian side. In fact, the Occupying Authority rarely abides by peace treaties with Palestinians that would slow down its occupation; on the contrary, since its occupation, it has never ceased its coercion, violent attacks, and forcible arrests and imprisonments of Palestinians. Therefore, the Oslo Accord was not different and did not enable Palestinians to establish a sovereign state, but it tied them with a security coordination agreement that caused divisions between Palestinians and augmented their socioeconomic suffering.

Presently, the occupying forces are still evacuating Palestinians from their homes by force of arms to build more settlements; as what has been happening in the neighborhood of Sheikh Jarrah in Eastern Jerusalem. Indeed, the Occupying Authority's, in 2021 its policies that it has woven to cause harm to the Palestinians through the 73 years of its occupation have bounced back on it. In retrospect, during the first and second Oslo Accords, the super power placed intense pressures on the Palestinians to sign a cession of 78 per cent of their lands to the occupiers and accept only 22 per cent of the total historical land of their country if they want to establish a Palestinian state to gain some independence. As for the two vital issues of Jerusalem and the return of the refugees to their homeland, the Occupying Authority did not want to decide on them, so it followed the method of delaying and stalling any decisions in reference to these two issues over the two years of negotiations from 1993 to 1995 until the accords were signed by suspending these two matters.

Moreover, the Occupying Authority's intention behind eschewing the discussion about eastern Jerusalem and the return of Palestinian refugees throughout the Oslo negotiations was on the one hand to prevent any increment in the census of the Palestinian population, and on the other hand, to occupy and implement their Judaization plans across the city of Jerusalem. The Occupying Authority's plan began with allegations and religious claims by settlers about the supposed temple that sits beneath the Aqsa Mosque. No trace of the temple was found, but that did not stop their excavational endeavors. Their real goal was not to find a temple, but to demolish a mosque.

In a Reuters article published in February, 2007 by Jonathon Saul, after an all-clear from the authority that no artefacts remain, the excavation work near an entrance to a compound in Jerusalem that houses al-Aqsa mosque resumes. The Occupying Authority's Antiquities Authority kept searching for artefacts at the base of the compound known to Muslims as Haram al-Sharif and its bulldozers broke up parts of the pavement at the foot of the ramp, damaged by a snowstorm and an earthquake in 2004, to clear the way for what the Occupying Authority calls a "salvage excavation" (Saul, Jonathan 2007).[31]

The current situation that erupted in April 2021 in the Sheikh Jarrah neighborhood in eastern Jerusalem, which in 1950 came under the rule of the Hashemite Kingdom of Jordan, also illustrates the Occupying

Authority's plan for Jerusalem. The Palestinian refugee families from the Western occupied part of Jerusalem and other occupied Palestinian cities of Haifa, Akko, Safad, Yafa, and other areas who left their cities were displaced by the Jordanian authorities into the houses that were owned by evicted Palestinians; who during the 1948 stampede were under the threat of the armed Zionist gangs and were forced to leave their houses in eastern Jerusalem and their homeland. However, these displaced Palestinian families are currently facing eviction from their homes that they lived in for sixty five years. The Occupying Authority's settlers, protected by their government's official forces, have been committing all kinds of infringements against Palestinian families to force their eviction from their houses and take their homes. Moreover, this eviction is supported by the Occupying Authority's Supreme Court that protects the crime of establishment of settlements by the government and the crime of home theft by settlers.

The Palestinians of the Sheikh Jarrah neighborhood refused to leave, and withstood the aggression of the settlers. The plight of Sheikh Jarrah became the main headline of various news bulletins. News of the Sheikh Jarrah neighborhood was spreading rapidly on social media and reverberated across the globe. Simultaneously, during the Muslim holy month of Ramadan, the occupying police forces invaded the Aqsa Mosque in large numbers, attacking worshippers with tear gas, rubber-coated bullets, and sewage wastewater. These invasions on Al Aqsa, in parallel with the evictions of Sheikh Jarrah families, mobilized thousands of Palestinian protestors. The protests grew, which caused several confrontations between the protestors and the Occupying forces used real weapons, shot some of the Palestinians in the head, and killed them; while the majority of the protestors were brutally attacked and arrested.

The evictions in Sheikh Jarrah and continued attacks on Aqsa Mosque prompted a response from Hamas, who lobbed locally manufactured missiles in rejection of the Occupying Authority's expansive and oppressive policies and the persecution of protestors. Hamas is a resistance group established in Gaza in 1988 and the legislative ruler of Gaza since its first electoral majority in 2006. The recent situation escalated to a comprehensive bombardment of Gaza, with air-strikes targeting commercial and residential streets, killing many civilians including up to seventy children, and causing severe damage to many factories, offices, schools, healthcare centers, and homes.

The establishment of settlements causes deteriorations in Palestinians' socioeconomic capabilities, specifically due to the loss of property, which has a grave impact on Palestinian lives and livelihoods. The occupation has been establishing settlements all over the occupied lands, including Palestinian territories. It aims at taking over the lands of Area (C) in spite of the Oslo Accords, which officially assigns this area as part of the Palestinian territory that was sectioned into three areas: (A), (B), and (C). The Oslo Accords, a peace treaty signed under the auspices of the international community, has been and continues to be repeatedly violated by the Occupying Authority, often under the guise of civilized terms, such as 'the development policy.'

As always, a network of crimes arises in parallel with this "development policy," which is essentially the ethnic cleansing of Palestinians from their lands. These supplementary crimes include the omission of the Arabic language from the occupied cities, alteration of land topographies, obliteration attempts for the Palestinian identity and culture, and fabrications of historical facts, to execute its Judaization policy. Hence, the settlement is a continuous occupying policy. The continuation of the establishment of settlements means that the small percentages left for almost half of the total population of occupied Palestine will keep shrinking.

Despite all the occupying entity's human rights violations and war crimes against the Palestinians, the world's superpowers, in particular the United States, continue to allow it to bypass accountability in all international forums. The US does not allow condemnation of the occupation by any other country to pass without refuting it with its veto. As a result, the establishment of settlements has sustained over 73 years, perpetuating a severe human catastrophe, while political, military, and financial support for the Occupying Authority's tyranny persists.

In international forums, Palestinians often stress the magnitude of their losses and the calamities they incur due to this particular occupative policy of settlement establishment. The Palestinians' demands are focused on ending this illegal construction of settlements on their lands by submitting to the international community all the needed evidence and clarifications of these crimes and their consequences. All the while, the Occupying Authority rarely abides by any treaty or agreement.

By and large, the United States' veto power permits the occupiers to disrespect all the United Nations' decisions and resolutions, concerning the establishment of settlements and all the crimes that precede this implementation and what precedes it, facilitate the reoccurrence of all these crimes, and empower the occupiers to go further in their Judaization policy. As a case in point, between 2016 and 2020 the administration of Ex-President Trump was a golden age for the Occupying Authority and its Prime Minister, who benefited from these four years at all levels by initiating the execution of new projects, such as the establishment of massive settlements that accommodate an additional 4,476 settlement units.

According to reports of the United Nations Office for the Coordination of Humanitarian Affairs (OCHA), which monitors the establishment of settlements, the settlements are being built on Palestinians' confiscated lands and in their territories, as is happening in different areas in and around the West Bank. For instance, OCHA monitored the establishment of a settlement in Hebron of thirty units. This small settlement, however, is established in the center of Hebron city in the Palestinian territories. The occupying government's policy allows the execution of settlement projects by any means. Then, in the pretext of protecting these settlements, it embezzles more of Palestinian lands to surround these settlements with buffer zones, such as the apartheid wall that detached most West Bank towns and villages, turned them into cantons, and tore them away from their cities and surroundings.

According to the Israel-Palestine conflict Aljazeera report that was published in 2021 under the title of Israel to build 1,300 settlement units in the occupied West Bank, the number of settlements has recently tripled since 2018 to reach 13,987. There has been a significant increment in the construction of settlement units to expand Jerusalem's settlements. In eastern Jerusalem, for instance, the settlement of Pisgat Ze'ev was expanded with American funding and support. The government of the Occupying Authority has adopted settlement plans that far exceed the number of settlements that the government agreed to abide by in 1992. An incident in 2021 brought these crimes to international attention on social media when a settler openly admits his crime in front of a camera, when he tells the Palestinian homeowner that if he doesn't steal her house, someone else will.

According to Wikipedia the process of *"Judaization,"* or *"Judaification"* is defined as "a process of cultural assimilation in which a person or a demographic group acquires Jewish cultural and religious beliefs and values. In August of 1897, the First Zionist Congress, held in Basel, Switzerland, planned to work diligently to Judaize the heritage of Palestinians and their Arab and Islamic culture. Since then, the process has been ongoing, and has become increasingly institutionalized. Many extremist religious groups are formed with the help of the Occupying Authority to accomplish Judaization through making alterations to certain religious and historical facts to be used for justifying the occupation and passing its occupative policies. British researcher Keith Whitlam, the author of *The Invention of Ancient Israel: The Silencing of Palestinian History* (1996), refers to this topic by explaining how historic information is changed to serve the political interest of the Occupying Authority. For example, the small kingdom of Israel, which was a relatively small and short-lived kingdom, is consistently referred to as a powerful kingdom that lasted for much longer than it did.

In its touristic pamphlets, the Occupying Authority points the printed datum in the direction it wants the Holy Land's visitors to think. For instance, many of these pamphlets display that the city of Jerusalem was established only in 3000 BC, ignoring 2000 years of its history to claim it as a Jewish city. However, the existence of Jerusalem dates back to 5000 BC, long before the Kingdom of David.

Various studies indicate that the Zionist movement pursued specific policies to penetrate the Palestinian territories, erase Arab names and replace them with Hebrew names with the goal of Judaizing the general landscape of Palestinian cities, towns, and villages as early as the late 1800s. The Occupying Authority's Judaization policies often target Islamic holy sites in Jerusalem with the aim of Judaizing the eastern side of the city with the intention to merge it to the fully occupied western side, and keep it under the control and authority of the Occupying entity.

The policy of Judaization continues as long as the occupation endures and visa-versa; safeguarding one maintains the other's continuity. Since its early days, the Zionist movement and its leaders espoused the policy of Judaization as one of the fundamental policies that facilitate marginalizing Palestinians, violating their rights, and plundering their properties. Furthermore, the Judaization policy is a brainwashing tool by which the Occupying Authority increases its gains through various methods that contribute to the fulfillment of the goal of prolonging its occupation. It is a tool of persuasion that the Occupying Authority uses to sustain Western governments' political support for its occupation and their financial subsidies to its army, and to control public opinion. Moreover, through this policy, the Occupying Authority obtains authorization to impose its illegitimate claim for a unilateral existence in Palestinian land and to falsify facts to keep embezzling Palestinians' properties. Therefore, Judaization is another technique by which the Occupying Authority preserves its unjust occupation of Palestine, and for the purpose of the Judaization of Palestine, it practices its unabated annihilation and ethnic cleansing against Palestinians.

Truth Telling in Cinema

"Cinema speaks in many different ways," said Shani, one of the directors of the film, T*he Ajami* (2009). The film's two directors, Scandar Copti and Yaron Shani deliver their film's message through candid scenes that depict the reality of the Palestinian condition under occupation. The directors shed light on more than one substantial issue: the socioeconomic statuses in Palestinian occupied cities, the subjugation of Palestinians under unfair rules and by coercive occupying forces, and the deterioration of Palestinians' general living standards due to imposed hardships, restrictions, scarcities, and lack of opportunities. The film communicates straightforward messages about the occupying policies and their consequences on Palestinian people. It also elucidates a political case that was deliberately complicated. The film revolves around a group of Palestinian youth living in Yafa, particularly in the Ajami ghetto; a neighborhood created to accommodate the Palestinians who survived the massacres and forced displacement of the occupying forces. What became a ghetto was named after the original Ajami neighborhood.

The directors of the film won several local and international awards, received a nomination for a "Best Foreign Language Film Oscar," and a special mention in the Golden Camera section at the Cannes Film Festival. According to film critics, although each of the film's directors associates with one of the two conflicting sides, the film delivers powerful messages and reveals some of the policies and practices of the occupying forces without triggering the tension between art-making and truth-telling.

In each of its scenes, *Ajami* underlines the destructive impact of the occupation, exemplifies how its policies affect the lives of many Inside-

Palestinian families, causing them deteriorations at all levels. The deterioration of Palestinians' socioeconomic statuses, for instance, is one of those aspects that the film stresses. The film poignantly illustrates how the imposed hardships by the Occupying Authority affect different individuals from different backgrounds, age groups, and religious affiliations. Moreover, the film focuses on the discriminative system of the Occupying Authority and how it discriminates against all Palestinians whether Muslims or Christians. Then, with the story of the restaurant owner, it implies how the Occupying Authority permits between Palestinians of both religions and distinguishes between them with certain allowances, favoritism, and other discriminative methods, such as providing the minority certain incentives while depriving the majority similar incentives. The Occupying Authority applies the old strategy of "Divide and Rule" between Palestinians since its occupation; thus, it emphasizes differences, stresses disunity, and keeps Palestinians engaged with side conflicts, applying other dividing methods to frustrate any possible effort toward unity and improvement, so it keeps them weakened from the inside to prevent them from struggling.

Through its story, the film depicts how some of the aforementioned occupative policies in this book are implemented against Palestinians. It demonstrates the consequence of these policies and their effect on the youth, such as the policy of decaying the Palestinian educational system and schools' curricula, the attempts of obliterating the Arab Palestinian culture, language, and identity, and the policy of impoverishment. The despotic authority implements these policies to keep Palestinian families vulnerable to different threats, hardships, implications, pressures, and diseases while depriving them of their basic rights, such as the right to health care, employment, and movement. The Occupying Authority divides Palestinian areas and maintains its hegemony with various checkpoints, barbed-wire fences, and the Apartheid Wall.

The film focuses on the occupying forces and officers' illegal practices against Palestinians, illustrates their involvement in spreading and encouraging crime and drug dealing among Palestinian minors.

Furthermore, the film's story expounds on how the occupying forces and officers follow a threatening method with one Palestinian group and tempting with money with another. Also, the film gives details on how police and security officers depend on the impoverishment policies to tempt Palestinian youths with illegal money to implicate them in drug dealing crimes. Then they shackle them with forced arrests and detentions, wherein they deprive them of a fair trial or any due process. On top of all these violations, the film shows how these officers issue verdicts and carry out punishments in the crime scenes. To exemplify all that in the Ajami film was an audacious effort that uncovered more than one of the repressive strategies by the Occupying Authority and its coercive controlling methods; as depicted in the film through the armed officers that showed up in the crime scene and killed the accused Palestinians, who were minors. What makes the matter worse is that this happens regularly, without the need for any evidence, away from legal procedures, and according to the occupying officers' discretionary judgments.

Besides documenting the socioeconomic deterioration in the Palestinian territories that is emphasized by high rates of unemployment and poverty and lack of education among the Inside-Palestinian youths, the story of the two teenagers and its disturbing ending added another dimension in revealing the life of the Inside-Palestinians under the ruling occupation. The disclosure of what happens on the ground in the occupied territories enhances the sincerity and realism of the film that shows how the Occupying Authority has an ad hoc legal system, which is applied to their liking on the Inside-Palestinians. The film also succeeds in depicting the illicit drug trade in the occupied Palestinian cities that are located behind the Green-Line, and revealing how they are in fact often planned by the Occupying Authority. The film focuses on the facilitation that the security and police apparatuses provide for the drug dealers, and how dealers are instructed to implicate young Palestinians, incriminating and distracting them.

The dilemma in the film's astonishing final segment is striking. After no drug dealer shows up, the two teenagers and the child realize that they fell into a trap. Suddenly, they find themselves under police officers' threat, who end up shooting and killing the eleven-year-old child and the sixteen-year-old teenager. Following this brutal scene, a flashback sheds light on the role of the third teenager; the eighteen-year-old boy who initially got in touch with the drug dealer, followed his instructions, and brought the small bag of drugs to the crime scene. However, after ending the lives of two children, arresting the third, and just before the final scene ends, the flashback reveals that the contents of the small plastic were not even intoxicants, but only a mixture of flour and powdered sugar!

Epilogue

The Occupying Authority's denial of its crimes and violations against Palestinians continues, but, during the latest attack of May 2021 on the city of Gaza and the unarmed Inside-Palestinians demonstrators, the world is better able to discern the authenticity and integrity of their claims. Many residential towers, buildings, farms, and trading centers were bombed and knocked down. On May 18th 2021, for instance, the Occupying Authority's air force and F-16 fighters dropped various types of bombs on Gaza's residential, agricultural, and industrial areas. according to NBC news reporter, Natasha Turak, "Israel's military reported that 62 of its fighter jets dropped 110 guided bombs onto the Gaza Strip overnight."

As a result, many families lost their homes, numerous buildings were destroyed, and the city's infrastructure was severely damaged. Over two hundred civilians were killed, many of whom were women, children, or innocent civilians. Entire families were wiped out. The Occupying Authority claimed that its attack against Gaza successfully targeted strategic Hamas locations. The barbaric airstrikes on Gaza were an alleged reaction to rockets lobbed on settlements by Hamas in reaction to the infringements of the occupying police and the settlers on the sanctity of the Aqsa Mosque, to stop their encroachment on the Palestinian families' right to live in the houses they own in Eastern Jerusalem, and to protest the brutal treatment and imprisonment of protestors. The Occupying Authority's response was clearly disproportionate as its air force carried out an intensive and deadly bombing campaign that lasted for eleven days.

Palestinians have endured over seventy decades of occupation and the Occupying Authority's ceaseless implementation of suppressive policies and human rights violations, and the ongoing levying of socioeconomic challenges on them to accentuate their deteriorated conditions and keep them marginalized and isolated. In addition, there is a severe disproportion between the occupying state and Palestinian popular resistance. Particularly empowering to the Occupying Authority's resources are the abundant subsidies it receives from the United States and other western countries and the political support it receives from these countries, often voting in its favor in international forums, or using the veto to annul any condemnation of the practices of the Occupying Authority, revoking any issued resolutions against it.

Moreover, the occupying power works hard to keep its practices against the Palestinians concealed, particularly from western populations. In order to achieve this goal, the Occupying Authority follows several methods, such as obfuscating news, fabricating and altering facts, and concocting historiography with tales that tell stories different from the reality of their occurrences, or based on undocumented information, in order to continue impacting western public opinion in its favor. For example, the story of the expulsion and displacement of hundreds of thousands of Palestinians, who were forced to leave their country in 1948 under the threat of arms, was narrated in a reversed way. The Occupying Authority's version of the story is neither compatible with its authenticated chronicles, nor with the registered memories of the Palestinians, who lived through the Nakba. The reversed version says that those hundreds of thousands of Palestinians were not expelled, but migrated voluntarily.

Undoubtedly, no matter how long the obfuscation endeavors last, the truth will be revealed. On the grounds that no one can deceive all people, not even some people, all the time. The wave of uprisings across Palestine in the spring of 2021 underlined a number of substantial facts: First, it proved that the Palestinian people did not forget that Palestine is the land of their ancestors and Palestine is their homeland, which they will never relinquish; as the Palestinian fourth and fifth Nakba generations have proven.

They also proved that the Occupying Authority's attempts to erase and abolish Palestinian identity, memory, and culture have failed miserably. The Palestinians' last uprising and unity that pervaded from the river to the sea and from Ras Al-Naqoura to the Negev Desert was phenomenal. They rose together to face the injustice, oppression, coercion, marginalization, and the guns and artillery of the occupying forces.

These uprisings, which came to be called the Unity Uprisings, proved to the world that Palestinians are ruled by a discriminative and racial system. The documentation of the incidents illustrated how the Occupying Authority treats Palestinians, and how it discriminates between them and its settlers and other citizens on the basis of race and religion. These incidents shed light on the Occupying Authority's policies of separating, isolating, and marginalizing Palestinians; it separates them from their surroundings, people, lands, and villages with checkpoints, barbed-wires, and its absurd Apartheid Wall.

The most recent uprisings and attack on Gaza also proved the failure of the occupative method of obfuscating facts and news, particularly in contemporary times, considering the shrewdness of the younger generations in matters of social media and technology. Today's youth are extremely comfortable with computers and search engines. They are internet savvy and they stay connected with the rest of the world through different social media channels that expose them to what is happening globally. This connectedness allowed transmission from the ground in Palestine with undeniable visuals, gravely challenging the effectiveness of the Occupying Authority's obfuscation method.

Finally, the most recent uprisings prove the validity of the known military statement that says: "The weak wins when the strong cannot break or defeat him," and underlines the philosophy of Friedrich Nietzsche, who said: "That which does not kill us makes us stronger."

It illustrated that believing in the justice of their cause made the Palestinians strong and armed them with the necessary political and ideological tools to continue their resistance. Moreover, their steadfastness added to their confidence and helped them to stay united and effective while facing the coercion, injustice, and discrimination of the fully armed occupying forces; despite their lack of firepower in the face of the Occupying Authority's great military might. Palestinians know that the occupying forces are not above harming, killing, and imprisoning them with little justification, but they also know that the occupying forces will always fail to defeat their tenacity, conviction, and determination to achieve liberation.

CONTENTS

Bibliography

1   Encyhttps://www.britannica.com/event/Siege-of-Acre-1799.

2   Satel, Abdel Qader 2018. Yafa: Fi Thilal Al-Nakba. Palestinian Occupied Territory: Qufur Qasem Press.

3   Mellaart, James 1965. Earliest Civilization of the Near East. London: Thames and Hudson.

4   Graetz, H. "History of Jews" The Jewish Publication Society of America, Philadelphia V. 1 (1891): p. 3.

5   Nakhleh, Issa 1989. The True History of the Land of Canaan. New York: Morning Star Press.

6   Jacobson, Dan 1982. The Story of the Stories. New York: Harper and Row, p. 30.

7   The Jewish Encyclopedia, p.1–6.

8   Shlaim, Avi 2007. Lion of Jordan: The Life of King Hussein In War and Peace. England: Penguin Books.

9   Bealey, Frank 2000. The Blackwell Dictionary of Political Science. Massachusetts: Blackwell Publishers

10 Pappe, Ilan 2006. The Ethnic Cleansing of Palestine. England: Oneworld Publications.

[11] Encyclopedia of the Palestine Problem 1991. Volume I & II. New York: International Books.

[12] AlJazeera. https://www.aljazeera.net/encyclopedia/events/2011/3/31

[13] https://www.aljazeera.net/encyclopedia/military/2015/5/14/1948

[14] Handala. http://www.handala.org/handala/

[15] Bastaki, Jinan 2017. "The Legacy of the 1951 Refugee Convention and Palestinian Refugees: Multiple Displacements, Multiple Exclusions Permalink." Berkeley Journal of Middle Eastern & Islamic Law, 8 (1).

[16] Le Vine, Mark 2005. Overthrowing Geography: Jaffa, Tel Aviv, and the Struggle for Palestine, 1880–1948. USA: University of California Press

[17] Chomsky, Noam and Pappe, Ilan 2015. On Palestine. Chicago, IL: Haymarket Books

[18] "Jewish ghettos in Europe" https://en.wikipedia.org/wiki/Jewish_ghettos_in_Europe.

[19] Noorulain Khawaja, April 27th 2018. "The Politics of Demography in the Israeli-Palestinian Conflict" Journal of International Affairs.

[20] "Jewish Immigration to Historical Palestine." *Factsheet Series No. 181, created: November 2013, Canadians for Justice and Peace in the Middle East*

[21] Daniel Estrin 2021. PNR "Israel moves ahead with settlements in sensitive locations surrounding Jerusalem" https://www.npr.org/2021/10/14/1045904263/new-israeli-settlement-projects-criticized-by-palestinians

22 Webinar "Colonization and Gentrification" by the US Campaign
    for Palestinian Rights:
    https://uscpr.org/ColonizationGentrification/

23 Sasson-Levy, Orna. 2013. "A Different Kind of Whiteness:
    Marking and Unmarking of Social Boundaries in the Construction
    of Hegemonic Ethnicity." Vol. 28, No. 1 (March 2013).

24 UN experts alarmed by rise in settler violence in occupied
    Palestinian territory GENEVA (10 November 2021).
    https://www.ohchr.org/EN/NewsEvents/Pages/DisplayNews.aspx
    ?NewsID=27792&LangID=E

25 B'Tsalem, October 2009. The Israeli Information Center for
    Human Rights in the Occupied Territories. "Without Trial:
    Administrative detention of Palestinians by Israel and the
    Incarceration of Unlawful Combatants Law."
    https://www.btselem.org/publications/summaries/200910_
    without_trial

26 United Nations Conference on Trade and Development,
    UNCTAD 2020 Report. "Assistance to the Palestinian people:
    Developments in the economy of the Occupied Palestinian
    Territory." Trade and Development Board Sixty-seventh session
    Geneva, Item 10 of the provisional agenda.

27 Steven Shepherd and Aaron C. Kay 2011. "On the Perpetuation of
    Ignorance: System Dependence, System Justification, and the
    Motivated Avoidance of Sociopolitical Information." Journal of
    Personality and Social Psychology by the American Psychological
    Association Vol. 102, No. 2, 264–280.

28 United Nations Development Program. "Arab Human
    Development Report 2003: Building a Knowledge society 2003.
    New York: UN Publications.

[29]   Constance Elam, 2002 "Culture, Poverty, and Education" Purdue University Press, 2002 Volume 18, No. 1 Spring 2002. Pp.10–13. https://docs.lib.purdue.edu/cgi/viewcontent.cgi?article=1484&cont ext=eandc

[30]   Amnesty International. Chapter 3. "Israel Settlements and International Law." 2019. https://www.amnesty.org/en/latest/campaigns/2019/01/chapter-3-israeli-settlements-and-international-law/

[31]   Saul, Jonathan 2007. "Israeli excavation in Jerusalem stirs Muslim Anger." https://www.reuters.com/article/us-palestinians-aqsa/israeli-excavation-in-jerusalem-stirs-muslim-anger-idUSL0624 826320070206

Printed in the USA
CPSIA information can be obtained
at www.ICGtesting.com
LVHW010838300124
770328LV00002B/207